The School-Savvy Parent

365

Insider Tips to Help You Help Your Child

by
Rosemarie Clark, M.Ed., Donna Hawkins, M.Ed.,
and Beth Vachon, M.Ed.

Edited by Marjorie Lisovskis

free spirit
PUBLiSHiNG®

Works
for kids®

Library of Congress Cataloging-in-Publication Data

Clark, Rosemarie, 1956–
     The school-savvy parent : 365 insider tips to help you
  help your child / by Rosemarie Clark, Donna Hawkins,
  and Beth Vachon.
       p.   cm.
  Includes index.
  ISBN 1-57542-072-4 (pbk.)
  1. Education, Elementary--Parent participation.
  I. Hawkins, Donna 1956– . II. Vachon, Beth
  1956– . III. Title.
  LB1048.5.C53   1999
  371.19'2--dc21   99-29793
                                         CIP

Cover design by Percolator
Book design and illustrations by Dao Nguyen
Index prepared by Randl Ockey

This book contains many recommendations for Web sites.
Because Web sites change often and without notice, we can't
promise every address listed will still be accurate when you
read it. When in doubt, use a search engine.

10 9 8 7 6 5 4 3 2

Printed in the United States of America

Free Spirit Publishing Inc.
400 First Avenue North, Suite 616
Minneapolis, MN 55401-1724
(612) 338-2068
help4kids@freespirit.com
www.freespirit.com

Dedication

To our families

Acknowledgments

Writing this book fulfills a dream. Now that the process is completed, we wish to offer loving thanks to many people.

From Rosemarie, thanks go to: My husband Danny, who is always there to love, encourage, and support me. My two precious sons Nathan and Sean, who make me so proud and who always had faith in their mom; their laughter and love have enriched my soul. My parents Bob and Sonja Knoerr, who gave me love, determination, and confidence. Mary Jo, who is both my aunt and my friend. My grandmother Alberta Knoerr, who showed me the way. And of course my partners in crime, Beth and Donna.

From Donna, thanks go to: My parents Evelyn and Elwood Smith, whose steadfast devotion and support give me strength and confidence. My children Sarah, Emily, and Jordan, whose energy and enthusiasm are my inspiration. I am so proud of you! My husband Mark, whose love makes me a better daughter, mother, teacher, and friend. Rosemarie and Beth, the friends I've shared my life with. I have been so blessed.

From Beth, thanks go to: My husband Kevin, for sharing my dream, strengthening my vision, and relishing the joy of success. My daughters Erin and Juliann, for believing in me, inspiring me all their lives, and making it easy to be a good parent. My parents Irvin and Gwen Lambert, who provided a strong foundation to grow on. My mother-in-law Edith Vachon, who always knew our book would be published. Rosemarie and Donna, for making our friendship a priority in their lives.

Finally, we want to thank the many parents, students, and fellow teachers who have taught us so much. Thanks to Caryn Pernu and Judy Galbraith for helping us jump through a teeny, tiny hoop to get published, giving us a chance to get our message out to parents everywhere. Margie Lisovskis was wonderful to work with and great at shaping the book into its best form. Thanks to Nancy Robinson, for all the terrific ideas to help others learn about our book.

On to the next dream.

Contents

Introduction 1

Back-to-School Tips 4

Home-School
Communication.......................26

Routines to Live By 42

Health and Safety 54

Homework and Tests...............74

Talents and Learning Styles 92

Setting Goals 106

Enrichment 114

Personal Responsibility 134

Getting Along with Others 148

Volunteering 164

Holidays and Breaks..............174

Index 194

About the Authors 198

Introduction

As teachers who are also parents, we understand the effort it takes to help children through elementary and middle school. We know that a strong connection between home and school can make a difference in whether and how children succeed in the classroom. Yet, to help guide a child to build a science project, memorize spelling words, practice math facts, or master study skills takes some know-how. It also takes time and energy—two things that, for many parents, are in short supply.

That's why we wrote this book. We want to make your child's school journey easier and less stressful for everyone—for your child, for the teacher, and for you. By sharing hundreds of strategies we've learned over the years in our classrooms and homes, we hope to help you find practical, positive ways to become an active, informed supporter of your child's education.

We invite you to use *The School-Savvy Parent* as a guide you can turn to again and again. It applies to children in a wide age range—from kindergarten through middle school. Because school is about studying and more, we've offered suggestions in a variety of areas, including basic skills, home-school communication, routines, planning, responsibility, enrichment, and "latchkey" issues. We've also suggested books, magazines, and Web sites that offer more in-depth information on many of the topics we cover.

Use this book however you'd like. Dip in to whatever chapter or topic interests you. If you want to read about a specific issue like test scores or safety on the bus, scan the index to find what you're looking for. Don't feel that you have to follow every tip. Take what you can use and leave the rest. Share the book with a friend, or even with your child's teacher.

We'd love to hear how our ideas work for you. We'd also like to learn about tips you have that could help other parents, if you'd care to share them. Please write to us at this address:

> Rosemarie Clark, Donna Hawkins, and Beth Vachon
> c/o Free Spirit Publishing
> 400 First Avenue North, Suite 616
> Minneapolis, MN 55401-1724

If you're online, you can write to us at:

> *help4kids@freespirit.com*

Keep up the great work you are doing raising the next generation. The time and effort you invest will pay off now and for a lifetime!

Rosemarie Clark
Donna Hawkins
Beth Vachon

Back-to-School Tips

Ready, set, go!

Q. *How can I get my child and myself off to a good start in the new school year?*

A. A little thought and planning can make all the difference!

Will your child be entering a new school or starting school for the first time? If so, call to arrange a tour. Visit while school is in session so your child can see the normal routine. Note the location of the classrooms, restrooms, cafeteria, library or media center, office, auditorium, and gym. Familiarity with the new school will help your child feel more at ease.

In many schools, parents are allowed to request a certain class or teacher. Find out your school's policy. If you can (and want to) choose, by all means do. Talk to parents in your neighborhood about teachers their children have had, or see if you can watch a class in session.

Some school systems offer choices among schools and programs. Call your school district offices to find out what your options are (for example, traditional, Montessori, open, or language-immersion programs). There may be deadlines or waiting lists. You may have to figure out special transportation. It's a good idea to begin thinking a full year ahead of time about what you want for your child.

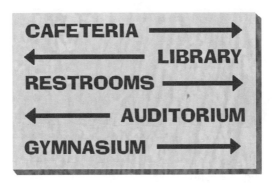

Many parents wonder if their child is ready to start school. Even the brightest child may not be ready for kindergarten at the age of five. Most kindergartens have children ages five, six, and seven. If your child will turn five close to the cutoff date, you may want to wait a year. Ask yourself: What are the pros and cons of enrolling my child now? Later? List all your ideas. Talk to the school psychologist or counselor about what will be best for your daughter or son.

If you're not sure your kindergartner is ready to go on to first grade, talk with the teacher. She'll be able to judge whether your child's skills and maturity level are in sync with those of other children.

FYI

Here are two books that might answer some of your questions about your child's school placement:

Kindergarten—Ready or Not? A Parent's Guide by Sean A. Walmsley and Bonnie Brown Walmsley (Portsmouth, NH: Heinemann, 1996). Topics include types of kindergartens, entry age, half day vs. full day, and advanced learners.

Is Your Child Ready for First Grade? by Eleanor H. Tilghman (Newark, DE: T.E.S.T. Inc. Publishing, 1998). Provides information on skills needed to succeed in first grade along with readiness activities and helpful checklists.

A familiar face makes school a friendlier place to be. If your child is going to a new school, find a neighbor child who will also attend. Invite the child to your home. Who knows? A friendship might grow before school begins.

Throughout the summer, talk casually about the upcoming school year. Open the lines of communication so you know what your child is thinking and feeling about school. Understanding what to expect may calm any worries or fears.

Ease the switch from vacation to school by setting bedtime a little earlier each night. Make it a goal to have your child on a regular bedtime schedule about a week before school begins.

Some children have trouble leaving home in the morning. To make it easier, send along a pocket-sized token such as a family picture, a corner of a beloved blanket, or a shell from an outing. Be firm and confident and say a friendly but quick good-bye.

It might take a little while for a comfortable relationship to develop between a child and teacher. Reassure your child that it takes time for people to feel at ease with each other. You might share a story from your own childhood about getting to know a teacher.

Your child may be missing a previous teacher or having trouble adjusting to a new one. Remind your child that every teacher has unique interests, talents, and teaching strengths. Ask how the new teacher is different and what's good about that. (For example, maybe eight-year-old Ramón misses all the songs Mrs. Trevino taught the class in first grade. But he likes the way his second-grade teacher uses lots of funny voices when he reads aloud.)

Expect your child's teacher to be professional, fair, and respectful. You should feel confident that the teacher cares about children, knows the subjects she is teaching, and welcomes parents' questions and concerns. Expect the teacher to send home graded papers and progress reports as well as information about when tests, projects, and events will happen. You have a right to expect high standards of your child's teacher. At the same time, remember that the teacher is only human. Don't expect perfection!

PROGRESS REPORT FOR

Alex Levedov

You are your child's first teacher. Your child is watching you and listening to you, so model a great attitude toward school. This positive cue from you can help school go more smoothly for everyone.

Before you buy any school supplies, call the office for a list. Teachers take care to list only *needed* materials that will fit into student desks. Your child may want mechanical pencils, a football pencil sharpener, college-ruled paper, or a super-size pencil box. Resist the urge to buy extra supplies—they're an added expense and often distract kids during class.

Buy school supplies early to take advantage of the back-to-school sales and the best selection. Large discount stores usually offer the lowest prices.

If possible, take your child with you when you shop for school supplies. Many kids love to shop for the things they need. This gets them excited about the start of school.

Older kids may want to shop for back-to-school items with their friends. Talk together beforehand about what your son or daughter needs and how much money is in the budget.

If you don't have a supply list, send your child to school with a backpack, paper, and a pencil with an eraser. These are the "tools of the trade."

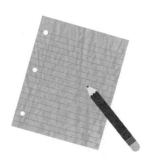

All supplies don't have to be new.
Last year's pencil box will work just fine.
Help your child feel good about recy-
cling a backpack or three-ring notebook.
It helps save money *and* the environment.

**If the supply list goes beyond
your budget, call the teacher or the
school's family resource center, counselor, or principal.** Ask which supplies
are optional and what assistance is available. You may qualify to pay lower fees
for supplies, sports equipment, or field
trips. In some cases, the school may be
able to cover these expenses for you.

Label everything—notebooks, folders,
calculator, and so on.

**The trail to and from school is often
adventurous.** Mittens may be lost.
Papers may be dropped. To help keep
materials safe, make sure your child has
a sturdy backpack. Label it, and check
that your child can work the zipper and
fasteners without any trouble.

If your child will buy breakfast or lunch at school, he will need a secure way to carry money, tickets, or a meal card. Many schools keep children's purchased meal tickets or assign an account code. This can be a big convenience all around. Check with the school to learn what will work best for your child.

Resist buying a *mega* binder that won't fit in the *mini* desks at most elementary schools. Folders hold paper nicely and take up much less space.

Compasses and protractors are usually inexpensive. If they are on your child's supply list, buy extras to keep at home for homework assignments.

It's best when school supplies stay at school. To keep art projects hassle-free, invest in two good pairs of scissors for your child—one for home and one for school.

Be sure your child's school clothes are "kid-friendly." Your child should be able to zip, button, tie, and fasten each item without help.

When buying shoes for school, keep practicality and safety in mind. Will the shoes be right for gym and recess? Slick soles increase the risk of skinned knees.

Many schools have a dress code. If your child is starting a new school, call the office ahead of time to find out the school's policy. One code might be simple (no T-shirts with profanity). Another might be more detailed (no skirts more than three inches above the knee). Choose clothing that fits the school's guidelines.

If you don't understand the reason for a dress code rule, ask. Some schools, for example, may forbid bandanas as a way to discourage gang affiliations. It helps if parents show support for the dress code—this way, kids are more likely to support it, too.

When it comes to school clothes, keep comfort and convenience in mind. Stay away from clothes that will distract or send an inappropriate message (such as bare midriffs, swastikas, or Confederate flags), even if these aren't specifically mentioned in a dress code.

If your child is supposed to wear a uniform, visit or call the school to see which clothing choices are most popular before you buy anything. For example, if most of the fourth-grade girls wear skirts rather than pants, your daughter may want to do the same. Finding out ahead of time can save you from buying items that won't get much use.

Check with the school to find out about any used-uniform sales and exchanges. You may be able to find low-cost items that have had very little wear. You can also sell the items that no longer fit your child. If no sales or exchanges are scheduled, why not suggest one? If you have time, offer to organize it yourself.

Shop early for uniforms in case you have to special-order a particular style or size. Shopping early is a good idea even if your child won't be wearing a uniform.

Kids tend to have a hard time remembering to wear a belt, which may mean they're out of uniform. Have your child store a spare belt at school in a desk, locker, or cubby.

To keep costs down, shop for school clothes at yard or tag sales and consignment stores. This is a good way to get quality clothing—and the latest style—at an affordable price.

Figure out transportation plans well ahead of the start of school. Will your child walk or bike to school? If so, make sure she's familiar with the route and understands safety rules. Will your child ride in a carpool? Why not invite the other kids (and parents) from the carpool to your home for a get-acquainted visit?

Many children get to school by bus. Before the first bus ride, help your child prepare by taking a ride on a city bus or visiting the school-bus garage. Bus schedules may be set weeks before school begins. Check with your district for the information you need. Tell your child the bus number. If you have a younger student, you may want to pin a tag with the bus number on it to your child's clothing. Review the number until you're sure it's committed to memory.

You and your child will probably be asked to review and sign a copy of the bus safety rules. If not, request an official list of these rules from the bus company or the school. Go over the rules together so you're surc your child is familiar with them.

If your child will take public trans-portation (a bus or train) to school, find a buddy, perhaps an older ele-mentary or middle-school child, to ride with your child. Before school starts, take time to ride the route with both kids, explaining their stops, where and how to buy tokens, and how to get help in an emergency.

Secretaries, principals, and other school personnel are usually at work before the first day of school. This is a good time to let them know about any medical condition your child has. It's also your chance to find out school policies on medication and care. Make sure the school understands your child's needs, as well as when and how to give needed medicine.

People at school need to be able to reach you during the day in case of an emergency. In addition to home and work numbers, share all other ways to reach you (cell phone, pager, fax, email). Provide numbers of other people the school can contact when you're unavailable.

If your child is injured or becomes ill at school and needs to be picked up, the school will contact you or another designated person. Take care in deciding who may check your child out of school. For safety's sake, only those listed may leave with your child, so make sure to provide enough names. Talk to the people you plan on listing to be sure that they're willing and able to help.

Keep your list of emergency contacts current. It's your responsibility to inform the school of any changes in your phone number or address—and those of everyone on your list. Be sure to let the school know when anyone on the list no longer has your permission to pick up your child.

Are your child's immunizations up to date? The school can tell you the federal and local requirements. Call early to arrange appointments for shots or physicals. Clinics usually schedule school physicals on certain days. The time slots fill quickly, so don't wait till the last minute. Some communities offer free or low-cost immunizations; call the school or your local health department for information.

Let your child's teacher know of any special holidays, customs, or practices that are important to you and your child. Does your family celebrate Rosh Hashanah, Ramadan, Christmas, Kwanzaa, or the Asian New Year? Is your child required to wear a special head covering? Are there foods your child shouldn't eat? Teachers will do their best to be respectful if they know what to expect.

Keep a list of key information that you can use when filling out forms. Different departments at the school need similar information, which is why it may seem like you're writing the same thing again and again. Here are some key pieces of information to keep handy:

- your child's social security number
- insurance information
- all phone numbers where you can be reached
- names and phone numbers of those who've agreed to pick up your child in an emergency
- names of medications your child takes regularly
- immunization dates

To stay organized at home, buy a different folder for each child. Use the folders to store permission slips, letters to and from teachers, school policies, or information about school events. This is especially important when you have children in different schools. Color-code the folders (green for one child, orange for another) so you know at a glance where to look for information you need.

Purchase or make a family calendar and mark school-related events (open houses, conferences, report-card days, days off, and so on). Display the calendar where everyone can easily see it. To encourage organizational skills, involve your child in updating the calendar on a regular basis.

On your calendar, circle your school's fall open house and make it a point to attend. Open house is a chance for you to meet the teacher and learn about your child's class. Bring along paper and pen to take notes. If you can't be there, call the school to set up an appointment to meet the teacher.

Start now to get your child in the library habit. Early in the school year, visit the library together (be sure to get your child a library card) and ask the librarian for a tour. Find out how to use the library's many publications and resources, including the different book genres, newspapers, reference materials, magazines, computers, computer software, videos, and CDs.

Home-School
Communication

Staying in touch

Q. *How can I communicate with the teacher about how my child is doing?*

A. Start early in the year, and keep in contact through good times and bad.

Early in the school year, teachers usually provide a plan for communicating with parents (for example, a monthly calendar or a weekly letter). Your child's teacher might explain this during an orientation meeting, through a get-acquainted letter, or at open house. Read or listen to the plan carefully. If something isn't clear, ask questions. Find out how you can get in touch with the teacher at school and when is the best time to call. If you're online, ask if you can reach the teacher via email.

If English isn't your first language, tell the teacher. Ask for the help you need to make communication between school and home clear. For example, you might request that letters to you be typed rather than handwritten, arrange to talk to the teacher in person instead of on the phone, or let the school know if you need an interpreter. Many schools have an ESL (English as a second language) or LEP (limited English proficiency) department. If yours doesn't, the school should be able to arrange for help through a community agency.

Conferences offer an opportunity for you to talk to your child's teacher one-on-one. You'll hear about your child's progress and have a chance to talk about any concerns. For convenience, many schools hold conferences during the day and the evening. If you can't go at the time that's been set, call or write a note to the teacher requesting a different time. Arrange to talk to "specialty" teachers as well as your child's regular classroom teacher. Art, music, and physical education teachers often have helpful insights about your child. And they like meeting parents, too!

WELCOME TO PARENT/TEACHER CONFERENCES!

When talking to the teacher, keep in mind that past records don't tell the whole story. Share information about your child's needs, feelings, strengths, and weaknesses as well as other concerns you have. For example, you may feel that your son's test scores are low because he gets very nervous about taking tests. Together, you and the teacher may be able to figure out a way to help your child feel less worried at test times.

I have a math test today!

You know your child better than anyone, and conferences give you a chance to share what you know. Don't be intimidated—the teacher wants to hear what you have to say.

If you need help interpreting test scores, ask for it. The teacher or guidance counselor can explain the scores and what they mean. Test results are only one way to measure your child's progress in school. The teacher may be able to give you more insight into how your child is doing overall.

The teacher can give you ideas for improving your child's test scores, if necessary. Ask the teacher's opinion of your child's performance in a weak area. Discuss how you can help improve your child's abilities and skills in subjects that present problems.

Where test scores show strengths, talk with the teacher about ways to encourage and challenge your child in those areas. Also ask how your child might best use his strengths to improve his school performance in subjects he finds more difficult.

FYI

Check out this book to learn more about testing:

School Testing: What Parents and Educators Need to Know by E.S. Gellman (Westport, CT: Praeger Publishers, 1995). Written for people with little or no training in testing, this is a great resource for anyone who makes decisions about a child's education. Explains the uses (and misuses) of tests.

Do you know what type of reading and math instruction your child is getting? Is reading taught through whole language, phonics, literature—or through a combination of all three? Is math taught using hands-on techniques? Does the class focus on a weekly theme? Are children grouped by ability? Ask questions to find out how your child is learning. Tell the teacher if you feel your child learns best in a certain way. (For instance, a child who likes to build models might be a hands-on learner. A child who likes to see an example might be a visual learner.)

Whenever you have a question or concern, write it down so you don't forget. Keep a list and take it with you to conferences. Bring a pen or pencil, too (it's amazing how many people forget this!). Write down the teacher's suggestions for helping your child at home, or bring a tape recorder so you can focus on the conversation yet still have the details.

FYI

For more ideas on making the most of school conferences, visit this Web page sponsored by the National Education Association (NEA):

"How to Make Parent-Teacher Conferences Work for Your Child." Offers tips on what to do before, during, and after a school conference. The page also has links to other sites of interest to parents. Web address: *http://www.nea.org/helpfrom/connecting/tools/ptconf.html*

Stay in touch with your child's teacher throughout the school year. Feel free to write notes, email, or call (leave a message with the office if you call during class). Teachers want to be "in the know." They appreciate hearing about parents' concerns, as well as getting the occasional compliment for a job well done.

Most schools welcome parent visits at nearly any time. Don't stop by unannounced when you want to talk about a specific concern, though. With twenty-five students, the teacher will be too busy to meet with you. Teachers also need to respect a child's privacy. Among those fifty ears, you can be sure some will be listening! Call ahead so you can schedule a time that's good for both of you.

Unless the teacher gives you a home number and invites after-hours calls, call her at school, not at home. Many teachers have voice mail or email at school (or you can leave a message with the main office). If you can talk only in the evening, let the teacher know; then arrange a time at night when she can call you.

If the teacher sends a weekly letter about what the class is doing or a personal note praising your child, display it where the whole family can see it. This reinforces the message that school is important.

Let the teacher know ahead of time if your son or daughter will need to miss school. If your child misses school unexpectedly, follow up with a note explaining the reason for the absence. Ask for a list of makeup work. After missing classroom instruction, your child may need extra help with this work.

Dear Mr. Andersen,

Anne was absent yesterday because of a family emergency. Please let her know what she needs to do to make up her work.

Thank you!

Mrs. Jones

Know the school's policy about how much homework children are expected to do. If in doubt, check the school handbook or call the teacher. Homework policies vary, and there's no one "correct" amount of homework. Typically, a school might assign 20 minutes a day for kids in kindergarten through third grade, 20–40 minutes for fourth and fifth graders, and 40–75 minutes for middle schoolers.

If you feel that your child spends too much time on homework, talk to the teacher about it. He may ask if your child does homework while watching TV, baby-sitting, or talking on the phone. You may want to ask if your child finishes work in class as quickly as most other students. Your child might need less work, or more help in settling down to do it. The teacher can help you figure this out.

Assignments that don't get turned in can be a big problem. If your child doesn't turn in all of her work, talk to the teacher together. Start by trying to find out why the work isn't being turned in. Does your child feel it's too hard? Is it so easy she just doesn't bother? Is she having trouble staying organized? Maybe she needs your reminders and supervision to make sure she's putting homework ahead of nonschool activities. Once you've gotten to the root of the problem, you can work together to find a solution.

One way to help a child stay on top of homework is to keep an agenda. Many teachers use agendas or planning calendars to help kids stay organized and to communicate with parents about assignments. Check your child's agenda every night. If the school doesn't use agendas, buy or create one yourself or with help from your child.

FYI

Here's a resource that can help the whole family plan for school and other activities:

Agendamate. A colorful erasable wall chart you and your child can use at home to plan homework and other daily and weekly "to do's." Premier School Agendas, 2000 Kentucky Street, Bellingham, WA 98226. Toll-free phone 1-800-447-2034.

If your child is having a problem at school, discuss it with the teacher first before going to the principal. Most teachers welcome the opportunity to work through a problem before it gets bigger. If you, your child, and the teacher can't solve it together, then you will need to talk to the principal or school counselor.

If the teacher isn't meeting your expectations, set up an appointment for the two of you to talk. At your meeting, tell the teacher your concerns. See if you can agree on a way to improve the situation. For example, if your child is struggling with reading and you don't feel he's getting enough help at school, discuss what the teacher is doing and ask what you can do.

If there are problems on the playground, in the cafeteria, or on the bus, your child should tell the adult in charge. That person (playground supervisor, lunchroom monitor, or bus driver) will know more than the teacher about what has happened and may take the matter to the counselor, assistant principal, or principal. (The "chain of command" varies in each school district.)

To follow up on a problem you, your child, and the teacher have talked about, send a short note that can be answered quickly. The teacher will appreciate this simple approach to keeping track of how things are going.

Dear Ms. Garcia,

Has Paul's attitude been appropriate this week? Is he turning in his work?

Yes   No   Comments?

Do you worry about the way your child acts or approaches schoolwork at home? Ask the teacher about the general traits and behaviors of children in this age group. He can help you decide if certain actions are typical and whether they might be cause for concern.

When you call the teacher or meet, introduce yourself and say whose parent you are, even if you've met before. ("Hello, Mr. Sophal. I'm Sara McBee—Maggie Cherne's mother. I met you at the open house.") An elementary teacher may have twenty-five or even thirty students and some middle school teachers up to four times that number, many with different last names than their parents. That's a lot of names to learn! Be patient if the teacher doesn't always remember yours.

Tell the teacher if your family is going through a difficult time. You don't need to go into great detail. The point is to let her know that your child is under some stress. This information will help the teacher understand your child's behavior and offer support.

You may want to confide in the school counselor, family resource center, or school social worker when your family is experiencing a crisis. If they can't help, they may be able to put you in touch with people or agencies that can.

Let the teacher know if you can't afford to pay for a field trip. Many schools set aside funds to help in this situation.

Take a minute to write a note of appreciation to a teacher who's doing a good job. We all like to hear words of praise and encouragement. Positive feedback tells teachers when their methods are especially successful.

At some point, a teacher may touch your child's life in a special way. When this happens, why not write the teacher a thank-you note? Give a copy of your letter to the principal, too. If you'd prefer, leave a phone message with both of them. The principal, dean, or headmaster is the teacher's boss. Positive feedback from parents lets this supervisor know when a teacher is doing an especially good job.

Routines to Live By

Day by day and
week by week

Q. *Our family is busy! When life is hectic, what can I do to help keep my child on track in school?*

A. Set routines and follow them—this is the key to keeping school manageable and rewarding for your child. Once routines become habits, they won't seem hard to follow.

Set a bedtime for your child. Stick to it during the school year, even in the spring when the days grow longer.

Aim for a consistent morning routine. Following a regular schedule for getting up, eating, and taking care of chores like walking the dog or making the bed will set the stage for a productive day.

Send your child off to school with a kiss, a hug, and the words "Have a great day—I love you!"

It's important for your child to be on time for school and to stay for the entire day. When kids arrive late or leave early, they may miss announcements or assignments and disrupt other students. Whenever possible, schedule doctor and dentist appointments during nonschool hours. This will make school go more smoothly for your child, the teacher, and you.

Valuable information may be waiting for you inside your child's backpack. Look through it together every night, checking for assignments or notes from the teacher. This will also give you a chance to make sure that the yogurt isn't spoiling in the bottom of the pack and that there's nothing inside, such as a pocketknife or cough drops, that shouldn't be going to and from school. (For additional tips about what items are not permitted in school, see page 64.)

Every day ask, "How did your day go?" Also ask what your child did at school. If the answer is "Nothing," ask more specific questions. "What are you learning about in social studies?" "How did your science experiment turn out?"

Conversation Starters:
Questions to Ask Your Child

Here's a starter list of questions that will help you get answers about your child's school habits, supplies, studies, and more. A word of caution: Ask only one or two questions at a time.

"Housekeeping" Questions
- How are you doing with keeping your (cubby/desk/locker) clean?
- How many pencils do you have? Do they still have erasers?
- Do you have all the (markers/colored pencils/writing paper) you need?
- Is the calculator working right, or is it time for new batteries?
- Do you owe lunch money or have any lunch charges? How much?

Questions About Getting Along
- How are you getting along with your teacher?
- Who are you sitting or working with at school?
- How are things going on the school bus?
- What do you do outside at recess?

Health Questions

- Do you wash your hands after using the restroom?
- Are you remembering not to share hats or combs?
- What are you eating at lunchtime?

Questions About Learning and the Learning Environment

- Are you getting used to your new (school/room/teacher)? How is it different?
- Can you see the board from where you sit?
- What's your favorite (subject/class) right now? Why do you like it best?
- What topic are you going to choose for your term paper?
- How did you solve the problem you were having with the (math/social studies/science/writing) assignment?
- Are you thinking about (joining band/playing a sport/trying out for the play)?
- What's the best part of your school day? Why?
- What's the hardest part of your school day? Why? What do you think would make it better?

Set a consistent homework time. Provide a quiet, orderly place where your child can study (such as a work area in the bedroom, a desk in the living room or den, or the kitchen table). Make it a rule not to let the phone, TV, or computer games interfere with study time. As your child settles into this routine, you might notice that more work gets done in a shorter time.

Remember to check your child's list of assignments every day. Don't accept excuses for why assignments and other important information aren't written down. If the teacher doesn't give assignment sheets or use a daily planner, you may want to give your child a small notebook for keeping track of assigned work.

Ask to see your child's schoolwork daily. Notice and comment on good work. Go over mistakes as well. If you feel review is needed, tell your child to bring textbooks home. If you're not seeing schoolwork on a regular basis, check with your child and the teacher to find out why.

Limit television time. In most cases, it's best to save TV viewing until after your child is finished with homework. Some children, though, might want a bit of downtime with a favorite after-school program before settling into homework or other activities.

Set aside planned reading time each day (the half hour before bed is a good time for this). Allow your child to choose what books or magazines to read at this time.

Remind your child to take care of daily responsibilities—for school and for home chores, too. Make your reminders friendly: "I don't think I've seen your vocabulary sentences yet." "Kitty looks pretty hungry." "Remember, you need to have your chores done by five o'clock so we can go to Grandpa's."

Help your child organize materials for school. Load and check backpacks at night before bed. Most older kids can do the organizing and packing on their own, but younger children need more help. You know your child best. Give help as long as it's needed. (For example, seven-year-old Irina and her dad load the backpack together. Tyler, who is ten, asks his mom to check his pack after he's filled it. LaShonda, an eighth grader, uses a checklist she made herself.)

Backpack Checklist

✓ Math book
✓ Science fair project notes
✓ Social studies homework
✓ Lunch money

Keep a copy of the school calendar with your family calendar. Plan family outings over school holidays and breaks. Some schools have rules about vacations while school's in session; others don't.

But all schools and teachers appreciate it when parents recognize how important it is for children to be in school every day. This also sends your child the message that you value education.

Take advantage of three- and four-day weekends to catch up on projects and missed or late work. If you haven't planned a family outing over a school break, encourage your daughter or son to spend some time on a long-term project or reviewing schoolwork. This will help your child stay on top of things and give some structure to time spent away from school.

Check every week or two to see if your child needs more school supplies such as paper, pencils, notebooks, calculator batteries, or markers.

Set aside some time each week to read together as a family. At times, you might each read your own books, but also take some time to read aloud. A shared book can be just as enjoyable as a game, TV show, or movie. You know it's good for your child to read—it's also good for him to hear other people read. Remember, the *more* your child reads, the *better* he'll read.

FYI

To make reading aloud fun for the whole family, you might try one or both of these books:

The Read-Aloud Handbook (Fourth Edition) by Jim Trelease (New York: Penguin USA, 1995). This highly acclaimed handbook describes how to set a great read-aloud atmosphere and recommends more than 12,000 titles—from picture books to novels—for families to share.

Read All About It! Great Read-Aloud Stories, Poems, and Newspaper Pieces for Preteens and Teens edited by Jim Trelease (New York: Penguin USA, 1993). Presents 48 works from books, newspapers, and magazines, including writings by Maya Angelou, Ray Bradbury, Roald Dahl, Gary Paulsen, Mike Royko, and more.

Eat together as a family as often as possible. Turn off the TV and turn on the answering machine. Use mealtime as a chance to talk about things that interest everyone in the family. (Save lectures or discussions about behavior problems for a different time and place.)

Don't give up if you slip from your routine. Sometimes people get sick. Sometimes school, jobs, and outside activities get so hectic that routines are temporarily forgotten. When this happens, get back on track as quickly as you can, and go from there. If your child has fallen behind, ask the teacher how you can help her catch up.

Health and Safety

Staying on the right track

Q. *How can I make sure my child stays healthy and safe when I'm not there?*

A. You can't guarantee that your child will never be sick or hurt, but you can help your son or daughter form healthy habits and provide your child with clear information about safety.

Healthy eating helps children be alert and do their best in school. Make good nutrition part of daily life. Plan meals using the Food Guide Pyramid, and teach your child about the pyramid as well. Stock the kitchen with healthy snacks like cereal, fruit, celery and carrot sticks, and yogurt.

FYI

The Food Guide Pyramid gives a helpful picture of how to choose foods from five major food groups. You can learn more about it by contacting the U.S. Department of Agriculture, 14th and Independence Ave. SW, Washington, DC 20250. Phone number: (202) 720-2791. Web address: *http://www.usda.gov/*

Encourage your child to eat balanced meals when eating away from home. Chat about what he's eating for breakfast or lunch at school. Are there choices? What offerings does your child like best?

Pack or help your child pack healthy lunches for school. Instead of sugary treats and sodas, include fresh fruit, cottage cheese, or whole-grain crackers. Surprise your child with a friendly note in the lunch box or bag.

Hi, Kate!

I sure enjoyed hearing your book report last night. Good luck with it today!

Love,

Dad

Make sure your child gets plenty of exercise each day. Exercise sharpens "brain power" and helps kids feel stronger and more energetic. Outdoor play and after-school activities like sports or dance are great forms of exercise. Your child can also get moving by walking the dog, vacuuming the living room, or carrying groceries up the stairs.

Set a bedtime that lets your child get plenty of sleep every night. Reading, listening to quiet music, or drinking milk can help ease a child into a relaxed mood.

Review the do's and don'ts of using the bathroom. (This is the one place at school where the teacher isn't always available to supervise.) Children often forget to flush the toilet or wash their hands at school.

Teach your daughter or son to respect the privacy of others in the restroom. Remind your child not to peek under the stall doors or splash others who are using the sink.

It can be hard for kids to keep from wiggling a loose tooth, but encourage your child to leave the tooth alone. Explain how easy it is to lose a tooth over the course of the day. Tell your child if the tooth does come out during school to ask the teacher for an envelope so it can be carried home safely for the Tooth Fairy.

From time to time, lice are a problem in most elementary schools. Teach your child not to share hats, combs, or brushes with classmates. This can help your child avoid getting lice or passing them on to other children.

Nosebleeds, paper cuts, and playground accidents often occur at school. Make it very clear that your child should not touch someone else's blood, bandages, or tissues. Explain that the best way to help is by quickly finding an adult who can handle the situation.

By around fourth grade, some kids need to wear deodorant. If this is true for your child, encourage him or her to use it each morning. Being teased about body odor is painful and embarrassing for a child.

Many girls worry about getting their period during the school day. Make sure your daughter is prepared in case this happens. Have her keep menstrual supplies in a zippered pocket of her backpack (be sure she knows how to use them, too). She doesn't have to tell anyone at school that she has her period unless she chooses to.

Your daughter should know what to do if her period starts at school and she doesn't have supplies. Together, identify adults in the school who will be able to help her. She might go to a teacher, a classroom aide, the school nurse, or someone in the office. Many girls feel more at ease talking to a woman about this issue.

If you live in an area where it's cold, "winterize" your child. Depending on where you live, hats, gloves, scarves, tights, long underwear, extra socks, boots, or raincoats may be essential gear for outdoor winter fun. Some schools have recess outside year round, so send your child out the door wearing clothes that fit the weather. Check to make sure he has all the extra warm things he'll need. Kids aren't always happy or willing to wear all the outdoor clothing they should. Talk to your child about this and remind him that dressing right helps him stay healthy.

When your child has a cold, sinus trouble, or allergies, send along a pocket-sized pack of tissues to school.

A child who has a fever, an upset stomach, flu, or a severe cold or cough should be kept home from school. Still, it's not always easy to know if a child is really sick. When the complaints don't seem too serious, you may decide to send your child to school. When you do, instead of saying "Have the school call me if you don't feel better," you might say, "Sometimes people feel better after they're up and going. I think you can make it through the day."

Send along a note in a sealed envelope for the teacher. He'll appreciate knowing what's going on.

Dear Mr. Skolski,

Scot said he didn't feel well today, but I suspect he's not really sick. I think he may be worried about our dog, who's about to have puppies. I thought I'd let you know, just in case.

Thank you.

Julie Hocksted

Does your child have nosebleeds or faint easily? Make sure adults in charge know about these things so they can handle problems without causing undue alarm over your son or daughter.

Ask about the school's medication policy. Find out if your child is permitted to carry medicines like cough drops or asthma inhalers to school. Bring over-the-counter or prescription medications to the teacher or office, and keep prescription drugs in the original containers with the pharmacy instructions and information about possible side effects. It's important to make sure the people who handle medicines know exactly what medicines your child needs to take as well as when, how, and why to administer them. (For example, a child may have asthma and need to take two puffs of an inhaler one hour before recess so he won't wheeze. A diabetic child who needs an insulin shot at exactly 1:00 P.M. might give herself the shot while the school nurse watches.) Keep track of when your child's school medicine supplies need to be refilled.

Kids who are old enough to be in school need to be talking with parents about the dangers of tobacco, alcohol, inhalants, and other drugs. Children need to know that they should never use any of these substances and that it's important to tell parents if anyone tries to get them to use drugs or other harmful things. Talk to school officials to learn what kinds of problems and education are going on in your school and community. Is there a concern about drug dealing near the school? Have teachers observed children sniffing glue? What and how does the school teach kids about healthy habits? Has a parent or community group been formed to address the issue of prevention? Equally important, remember that when it comes to drug-use prevention, you are the most important role model for your child.

Discuss safety rules regarding fireworks. Make sure your child knows how to use them safely and that an adult should always be present. Know the law, too. Fireworks are illegal in many parts of the country. Whatever the law, it's never okay to bring fireworks to school.

Tell your child it's not okay to fight, kick, hit, pinch, name-call, or swear. Teach your child to try to work out problems by talking or to walk away. (See page 162 for resources on the subject of bullying.)

Make sure you and your child know the school's weapons policy. Most schools have zero-tolerance rules about dangerous items that may be brought to school. A child could be suspended for having a small pocketknife or even a squirt gun inside a backpack.

If you have a weapon in your home, be sure it's unloaded and kept under lock and key. Store ammunition separately and lock it away, too. Teach your child gun safety rules. Above all, tell your child he is *never* to touch any weapon when you are not with him. This will help prevent your child from being hurt or harming someone else at home or at school.

Make sure your child has a safe way to get to school. If the route is dangerous, walk with your child, give her a ride to school, or arrange for an adult you trust to do this.

Go over traffic safety rules with your child. Even older children need to be reminded to cross at crosswalks, follow signals, obey school crossing guards, and look both ways.

Remind your son or daughter to buckle the seatbelt when riding in a car. Don't count on your child, or the driver of the carpool, to remember this. Children have other important things on their minds, like the new gerbil waiting at home, the ballgame after school, or the party Saturday night.

Teach your child safety rules for riding public transportation. (For example, don't try to get on the subway when the doors are closing. Take a seat if possible, and hold tight to a handrail if there isn't a seat.)

Does your child have safety equipment at home *and* school? Bike helmets, wrist and knee pads, mouth guards, and other safety equipment protect your child during sports and play.

If your child argues about wearing a helmet, life vest, or seatbelt, say, "I love you too much not to insist on the safe, responsible thing to do."

Sign up for swimming lessons. If your child had them last year, see if there's another level to take. Swimming is not only fun—it's a lifelong skill. Instruction and practice can help protect your child from unnecessary danger around water.

If your child will be staying alone during the day over an extended school break, check with your medical provider, the Red Cross, or a community education program to see if they offer safety classes for children. Sign up your child for first aid or baby-sitting lessons.

As the seasons change, so do the safety rules. Remind your child about staying safe at school and on the way to and from. For example, in the fall, remind your child not to play in leaves by the curb. In the winter, talk about when it is and isn't safe to walk on ice. In the spring, caution your child about the danger of flying kites near power lines.

Fire safety is important at school and at home. Teach your child what to do in a fire emergency. This is especially critical if your child is ever home alone or with a sitter. Schools hold fire drills throughout the year. Why not do the same at home? Have a fire escape plan that outlines how family members exit your home and where to meet once they're outside. Practice so everyone knows the escape plan.

Get your child into the fire safety habit by replacing smoke alarm batteries together. Do this twice a year when you set the clocks ahead and back.

Encourage your child to ask you "what if?" questions about a fire emergency. ("What if I come home alone and smell smoke in the kitchen?" "What if I'm in the bedroom and I can't open the door?") If you don't have a ready answer, figure one out together.

FYI

Share and talk about this book with your child:

What Would You Do? A Kid's Guide to Tricky and Sticky Situations by Linda Schwartz (Santa Barbara, CA: The Learning Works, 1990). A commonsense guide that prepares kids 8–12 to handle unexpected, frightening, and puzzling situations at home, at school, and on their own.

Contact the local fire department for information on setting up a home fire-safety plan that will meet your family's needs and answer your questions.

Have a safety plan for dealing with weather emergencies (tornadoes, blizzards, hurricanes) in your area. A local TV or radio station will be able to help you find information about this.

Does your child know what to do if he comes home and you're not there? Your child needs to know where to go and what to do in this event. You may have a neighbor who is home during the day and willing to be your emergency backup. Some communities have McGruff houses or other established safe homes where an adult has volunteered to be available for children who find them-selves alone or afraid. Check with your local police department to see if there's a program like this in your area.

Before deciding to have your son or daughter stay home alone after school, ask yourself if your child is ready for this responsibility. A child who feels worried or unsure about it *isn't* ready. Arrange for a sitter or seek out an after-school or community latchkey program.

Set guidelines about who's allowed to come in the house or apartment and where your child is permitted to go when a parent isn't home. If possible, call home from work or have your child call you upon arriving home from school. Touching base by phone will reassure both of you.

Find out if the school offers before- and after-school programs for kids whose parents work during those hours. If it doesn't, talk to school officials and other parents to learn how to go about starting a latchkey program.

Teach your child how to make an emergency call. (In most U.S. communities, dial 911.) Be sure your child knows her full name, complete address and phone number, and *your* full name. If your home is close to the school, your child should be able to tell someone how to get from school to home. Teach her a simple route using familiar landmarks. This could help if your child were hurt or in an accident.

If your child will *ever* be home alone, review emergency procedures frequently.

Get to know the work and travel schedules of other parents in your neighborhood. Be sure your child is not visiting a home where there is no adult present.

FYI

Read one of these books for other ideas about keeping your child safe when you can't be at home:

Disaster Blasters: A Kid's Guide to Being Home Alone by Karin Kasdin and Laura Szabo-Cohen (New York: Avon Books, 1996). Offers practical advice on caring for younger sisters and brothers, getting help, and handling emergencies.

Teaching Your Child to Be Home Alone by Earl A. Grollman and Gerri L. Sweden (New York: Lexington Books, 1992). A book written for members of "latchkey kid" families to read together. Covers a wide range of subjects including loneliness, illness, emergencies, and using public transportation. Includes checklists for preventing and handling problems.

Your child needs to know what to do if a stranger approaches at school or anywhere else. Remind your child not to talk to strangers, and to run to a safe place and get help from a trusted adult. It's important to discuss this often, even though it might frighten your child. Kids, even older ones, need to be reminded again and again.

FYI

To learn more about keeping your child safe from strangers, contact this organization:

The Child Connection, Inc.
2210 Meadow Drive, Suite 28
Louisville, KY 40218
(502) 459-6888
Web address:
http://www.childconnection.org

Homework
and Tests

Getting down to business

Q. *How can I help my child with schoolwork? I'm not a teacher, so I'm not always sure what to do.*

A. Your child does need your help, but you don't have to be an expert! You can help best by making school-work a priority and working to build good study skills.

Show your child that you think education is important by regularly asking how school is going. Find out what your child is learning and which subjects he likes best. Arrange a quiet, well-lit place for him to study and help him plan time to do homework every day.

Tell your child to start with the hardest assignment. Getting the most difficult task out of the way first is not only a helpful study habit but also a good life skill.

Don't feel bad about reminding your child to study. Most parents need to remind their kids to bathe, clean their rooms, eat right, and get proper rest. Kids need the same gentle-but-firm push when it comes to homework.

Help your child with specific skills when this help is needed. For example, your son might be having trouble with his math homework because he doesn't know all of his multiplication facts. You can help by drilling him on these facts every night.

If you and your child don't under-stand an assignment, attach a note asking the teacher for help.

> Dear Mr. Teng,
>
> I'm having trouble helping Emma figure out how to solve word problems. Could you please send me a few suggestions? Thanks!
>
> Sincerely,
>
> Bob McCoy

If you don't know how to help your child with a subject, ask someone else to step in. A grandparent, an aunt or uncle, a brother or sister, or a neighbor might be willing to help out. Check to see if the school, the library, or a community organization like the Boys or Girls Club can provide homework help through an after-school program.

Is there a homework hotline in your community? Call and learn what types of help it provides. Then encourage your child to use the hotline, and use it yourself when you need help assisting with schoolwork.

FYI

If you're online, visit these sites for homework help:

"Ask Jeeves for Kids!" At this search site, kids can ask questions in their own words ("Why did dinosaurs become extinct?") and get back links to resources that have answers.
http://www.ajkids.com

"Homework Central." Organized by grade level and topic, this site points the way to tons of resources.
http://www.homeworkcentral.com

"B.J. Pinchbeck's Homework Helper." Created by an elementary school student and his dad, this site boasts a huge collection of links to resources on a wide variety of topics.
http://www.bjpinchbeck.com

When your child's grades aren't as high as you'd like, try to uncover the reason for the problem. Ask yourself: Is my child studying regularly? Does she finish homework? How well does she understand what she reads? Share your thoughts with the teacher. Together, you may be able to find new ways to tackle the problem.

REPORT CARD

FOR _Maria Reynolds_

Art	B
English	C+
Math	C-
Physical Education	B+
Science	B-
Social Studies	A-

Many parents feel that they have a "weakness" in one subject or another. They assume that since they struggled with something in school, their child will, too. But the ability to learn a given subject doesn't necessarily run in families. If math (or science or grammar) isn't your strong suit, don't tell your child, "I never understood math."

He may decide that he's not capable of learning math either—or that you don't believe he is. Instead, let him know that you believe he can learn it. Review his daily work, give needed help when you can, and look for outside resources when you can't. The teacher may suggest some different ways to study, pair your child with another student, or recommend a classroom tutor. Many communities also have volunteer or paid tutoring programs available; call the teacher or school counselor for more information.

When your child has trouble with a particular subject or skill, let your words and actions show that you believe she can master it. If your child hears you say that she's "never been good at spelling" or that "geography isn't her subject," she may start to believe this. While students may excel in some areas and not in others, everyone needs basic skills in a variety of subjects. Tell your child you can get her the help she needs to learn difficult material. Follow through in supporting her. This sends a positive message—that she's capable of overcoming problems.

FYI

Check out these books on helping kids with homework:

How to Do Homework Without Throwing Up by Trevor Romain (Minneapolis: Free Spirit Publishing, 1997). Valuable insights, truths, and pointers are presented in this humorous book for kids ages 8–13.

How to Help Your Child with Homework: Every Caring Parent's Guide to Encouraging Good Study Habits and Ending the Home-work Wars (Revised and Updated Edition) by Marguerite C. Radencich, Ph.D., and Jeanne Shay Schumm, Ph.D. (Minneapolis: Free Spirit Publishing, 1997). Written by teachers, this book includes the latest information on helping children ages 6–13 with reading, math, science, and social studies; promoting critical think-ing; using technology; and developing study skills.

Be sure you and your child under-stand the classroom grading policy. Is a grade of 90 percent an A, or a B? What is the difference between "rapid progress" and "steady progress"? Ask the teacher to explain anything that's not clear.

To help your child keep abreast of ongoing assignments, post a calendar on the refrigerator and mark it with the due dates of special projects.

Large projects are more satisfying when tackled bit by bit rather than all at the last minute. If your child has a long-term assignment, set up a calendar outlining steps that must be taken (research, purchasing art supplies, writing, and so on). Have your child cross off each step as it's completed. Offer reminders about the project—kids forget easily.

Talk together about the help your child may need on a long-term project. While younger children usually require more help than older children, most kids will need some assistance at different points along the way. For example, with a fourth grader, you might help break down a research paper into smaller sections and set dates for completing each section. With a seventh grader who needs to plan a science project, you could help in gathering materials, talking through the steps involved, and asking questions that will guide the child.

Don't worry if your elementary-aged child counts on his fingers. A child who is learning basic addition and subtraction often finds fingers very helpful.

Teach your child to *count on* when solving addition problems. For example, to solve the problem 9 + 5 = n, have your child touch her fist to her chest and say the larger number, nine (9). Next, have her use her fingers to add the other five digits. The first finger makes 10, two fingers are 11, three are 12, four are 13, and five (including the thumb) are 14. She stops at five fingers, because 5 is the number she is adding to 9.

Help your elementary child master math facts. Addition, subtraction, multiplication, and division facts are the building blocks for higher-level math skills. Use learning tapes, flash cards (you'll find these at children's bookstores and in many supermarkets, or you can make your own), or handouts from the teacher to work with your child. Review the facts from time to time, even if you feel your child knows them well.

FYI

Another way to help with math facts is by using a musical math tape. Music and math are related in many ways. With our fourth graders, we use the tape *Multiplication Motivation* (younger and older kids will enjoy it, too). Write to Melody House Publishing, 819 NW 92nd Street, Oklahoma City, OK 73114, or check at a children's bookstore. Toll-free phone: 1-800-234-9228.

Children who use calculators a lot can become dependent on them. Every so often, check to see if your child is able to do basic math (adding, subtracting, multiplying, dividing) using only a pencil and paper.

Have your child read aloud to you often. Teach him that punctuation marks are like road signs. A period means to stop—the voice should go down. Commas mean to pause. Tell your child to visualize the story in his mind as he reads, like a movie. Stop him and ask him to talk about what he's read and predict what will happen next. ("Why did the boy feel so sad?" "What do you think the grandmother will say?")

Tell your son or daughter to skip an unknown word and read to the end of the sentence. With the rest of the sentence as a clue to meaning, your child can use letter sounds to try and figure out the unfamiliar word.

Keep a small paperback dictionary on hand. When your child can't figure out what a word means, it will be easier to look up if there's no need to lug a big book from the shelf.

When your child asks you questions that require a textbook to find the answer, teach her to use the book's table of contents, index, and glossary.

For a lengthy reading assignment, help your child set a certain number of pages to read per day.

FYI

You'll find helpful ideas on encouraging and supporting reading in this book:

99 Ways to Get Kids to Love Reading: And 100 Books They'll Love by Mary Leonhardt (New York: Crown, 1997). The author, a longtime English teacher and reading specialist, offers simple, practical tips to help kids learn—and love—to read. Includes a section on books for special interests such as horses, computers, or rock bands.

Check to see that your child is reviewing what he learns in science and social studies. These subjects usually require extra study in the intermediate grades. The concepts get more difficult, and kids often don't do well on assignments unless they devote some regular homework time to them. Have your child study by rereading, going over any notes he's taken, and reviewing vocabulary and study questions.

Quiz your daughter or son on the facts in the social studies or science book. Also ask your child to describe processes or experiments. ("How do rivers and harbors help urban areas grow?" "Can you explain how a bill becomes a law?" "What happens to make the leaves change color?" "What's happening with your science project where you're growing plants in your locker and on the windowsill? Why do you think you're getting those results?")

Simple hands-on activities can make science come alive. These activities can fill in the gaps caused by lack of experience and can help children understand the world around them. For example, if your child is studying the parts of a flower, take a flower apart. Compare the actual flower parts to the picture or diagram in the book.

FYI

Bookstores, toy stores, and the library are full of science activity books. Here are two your child (and you) might enjoy:

50 Nifty Super Science Experiments by Lisa Taylor Melton, Eric Ladizinsky, Michelle Ghaffari, and Neal Yamamoto (Los Angeles: Lowell House, 1997). Entertaining and challenging, these activities provide simple instructions and easy-to-follow diagrams.

101 Things Every Kid Should Know About Science by Samantha Beres, illustrated by Arthur Friedman (Los Angeles: Lowell House, 1998). A reader-friendly book that presents hands-on activities and entertaining facts about a wide variety of topics from cells and fungi to earthquakes and steam engines.

Spelling tests aren't just for Fridays anymore. Challenge your child to prepare throughout the week. A good way to do this is to write the difficult words correctly several times each night. Have your child look at each word, say it, write it, and check it for accuracy.

Use travel time in the car or on the bus to review textbook questions and practice math facts, spelling words, and vocabulary for English or a foreign language.

¿CÓMO ESTAS?

GUTEN TAG

SAYONARA

Many kids race through tests fearful of being the last to finish. Explain that faster doesn't necessarily mean better. Suggest that your child use any leftover time to review answers or double-check difficult questions.

Ask your son or daughter to bring home textbooks two or three days before a test. Help your child review test material by asking questions from the book or study guide. This will help your child be organized and better prepared by focusing on the important information in a chapter.

Keep in mind these test-taking basics: Your child will perform better on tests with a good night's sleep and a nourishing breakfast (and lunch if the test takes place during the afternoon).

FYI

Here's a book that can help your child survive (and even thrive!) when taking tests:

True or False? Tests Stink! by Trevor Romain and Elizabeth Verdick (Minneapolis: Free Spirit Publishing, 1999). A humorous kids' book that offers advice about overcoming test anxiety, procrastination, and perfectionism along with strategies for taking multiple-choice, true-false, timed, and take-home tests.

Talents and Learning Styles

Building on strengths

Q. *Why are some subjects and assignments harder for my child than others? How can I help?*

A. Each child has particular aptitudes, interests, and ways of learning. Recognize and build on those, and seek the school's help with problem areas.

Help your child discover and appreciate his special talents. Every child has unique talents and skills. Maybe your child draws clever cartoon characters, has a knack for computers, or shines on the basketball court. Or maybe he makes friends easily or leads and organizes others. Notice what your child likes and does well, then focus on these strengths. Encourage your child to make the most of them.

Children need extracurricular activities to help them build confidence and self-esteem. These activities offer a great way to support your child in building her talents or interests. Sign her up for programs at a local science museum. Enroll her in softball or soccer. Get her involved in scouting, music, or crafts.

Everyone has a particular *learning style.* Observe how your child learns best. For example, perhaps your son remembers what he reads out loud more easily than what he reads silently to himself. If so, he might be an auditory learner—one who learns best by hearing. Or maybe your daughter handles tests better after talking through concepts with someone else rather than reading or writing about them on her own. This is an interpersonal style of learning.

Present information in the way your child learns best. For some kids, seeing how a word is spelled may not be as helpful as actually writing the word down. While some children understand math concepts by doing written work, others might need to see or draw a picture of how square feet combine to form square yards, or use blocks to understand cubic measurements.

Regardless of your child's preferred learning style, the more senses you can involve, the better. For instance, if your child is studying the physical features of a region, have him look at photos of the mountains, plateaus, knobs, hills, and plains. Next, have him use clay or Play-Doh to make a relief map of the area. Ask him to explain the map to you and describe its features. Using three senses—sight, touch, and speech—will increase your child's chance of understanding and remembering what he's learned.

FYI

To find out more about learning styles, check out the following book:

Every Child Can Succeed: Making the Most of Your Child's Learning Style by Cynthia Ulrich Tobias (Colorado Springs, CO: Focus on the Family, 1999). Offers clear, sound ideas for supporting children's strengths and helping them meet their potential.

Let "Mistakes are okay" be your family motto. We all make mistakes. If children don't feel free to make mistakes, they're less likely to try new things. Sometimes, too, kids who fear they'll be reprimanded for mistakes decide to keep quiet or lie rather than risk admitting that they goofed. When your child makes a mistake, react matter-of-factly: "Oops. Looks like something red got mixed in with the socks and underwear. Won't we all be pretty in pink?" "Wow, that's quite a sunburn. It looks like you forgot your sunscreen." Teach your child that each mistake is an opportunity for learning. Ask questions like: "What did you learn by not following the directions?" "What will you do next time?"

Urge your child to ask questions in school. Some kids are naturally shy; others worry about what kids in class will think of them. Teach your daughter or son that there's no such thing as a "stupid" question. In fact, not asking can lead to problems later if your child hasn't understood something in a lesson.

Encourage your child to do her best. At the same time, guide her to look for ways to solve problems she has with schoolwork. If your child gets a low grade on a test, ask what she thinks the problem was. Did she spend enough time studying? Did she pay close attention during class? If so, brainstorm ways to bring about success. Your child may need help with a specific topic, like long division. Or she may need tutoring to keep up with daily work.

Praise your child every day. Be sincere—children know empty praise when they hear it. Focus on your child's strengths, interests, efforts, good deeds, and real accomplishments: "I love to see how much fun you and the puppy have together. You're a real dog lover, aren't you?" "Thanks for reading to your little sister. She sure admires her big brother." "Wow! You got a B+ on the Spanish test— way to go! It feels good to work hard and see results, doesn't it?"

Be specific when you comment on your child's artwork. A focused, positive comment ("Look at the detail you put into that car!") usually means more than a general one like "That's good."

Display samples of your child's schoolwork throughout the year. Hang them on a bulletin board or refrigerator, and when you're ready to take them down, store them in a special box, folder, or scrapbook. Your child will enjoy looking at them again and again and will take pride in the hard work and progress they show.

Frame artwork that your son or daughter brings home from school. Decorate your child's room with these "masterpieces."

Talk to the teacher if your child is having difficulty with schoolwork. Don't assume the problem will resolve itself as your child matures. It's true that much of learning depends on a child's level of development. Still, it's important to find the cause of a problem. Your child may benefit from extra time with the teacher, a different teaching approach, tutoring, or evaluation for special services. The teacher can help you figure out what steps to take.

FYI

Here's a good resource to look at if your child is having trouble with schoolwork:

Finding Help When Your Child Is Struggling in School by Lawrence J. Greene (New York: Golden Books Publishing, 1998). Gives tips for actions parents can take when a child is having difficulty with schoolwork. Addresses learning, attitude, and behavior and shows how to work within the educational system—or go outside the system when appropriate.

If you suspect your child has LD (learning differences), talk to the school to get help. Start with the teacher. Also check with the school psychologist, special education director, or student caseworker. A checkup at the doctor can be very helpful in identifying physical causes, such as hearing loss or vision problems, that may affect learning. Trust your instincts: you know your child better than anyone. If you believe there's a problem, persist in finding help.

FYI

To find out more about learning differences (LD), check out these resources:

The Learning Differences Sourcebook by Nancy S. Boyles, M.Ed., and Darlene Contadiono, M.S.W. (Lincolnwood, IL: NTC Contemporary Publishing Group, 1998). A resource to help parents and teachers identify and evaluate the best home and school environment for a child with a learning difference.

When Your Child Has LD (Learning Differences): A Survival Guide for Parents by Gary Fisher, Ph.D., and Rhoda Cummings, Ed.D. (Minneapolis: Free Spirit Publishing, 1995). Explains five types of LD and offers some possible causes, early warning signs, and lots of sound advice and information.

The School Survival Guide for Kids with LD by Rhoda Cummings, Ed.D., and Gary Fisher, Ph.D. (Minneapolis: Free Spirit Publishing, 1991). A book to help kids understand learning differences, build confidence, and make learning easier and more fun. Includes subject-area strategies and tips on taking tests, finding help, sticking up for yourself, and more.

Seek help if you feel your child is gifted. Many schools have programs for gifted children. The term "gifted" can have a broad meaning. Most schools identify gifted kids with academic talents, but your child may show advanced ability in other areas such as creativity or leadership. One gifted child might love to solve word puzzles or math problems; another might take apart clocks and radios to see how they work. Some gifted children ask many complicated questions and seem to understand complex ideas. Others might make architectural drawings, compose music, figure out elaborate football plays, write stories, sing, paint, or dance. Ask the teacher to recommend resources to help your child develop specific talents.

FYI

Here are some helpful books for gifted kids and their parents:

The Survival Guide for Parents of Gifted Kids: How to Understand, Live With, and Stick Up for Your Gifted Child by Sally Yahnke Walker (Minneapolis: Free Spirit Publishing, 1991). Full of information on giftedness, gifted education, challenges for parents and kids, and advocating for your child in school. For parents of children ages 5 and up.

The Gifted Kids' Survival Guide For Ages 10 & Under (Revised & Updated Edition) by Judy Galbraith, M.A. (Minneapolis: Free Spirit Publishing, 1999). A classic introduction to giftedness offers kid-friendly, practical tips, including "10 Ways to Make School More Cool," "4 Great Ways to Turn On Your Brain," and "The Perfection Infection (and Cure)."

The Gifted Kids' Survival Guide: A Teen Handbook (Revised, Expanded, and Updated Edition) by Judy Galbraith, M.A., and Jim Delisle, Ph.D. (Minneapolis: Free Spirit Publishing, 1996). Discusses IQ, goal setting, assertiveness, ethnic issues, stress, and more. For kids 11 and up.

Knowledge is power. If you think your child needs any special services, seek out information. Start by checking with the special education director. Learn what's available and how to take advantage of it. Keep a notebook and write down who you talked to, when you talked, and what you discussed.

Never give up on your child. He can only believe in himself if he knows that you believe in him. If you feel discouraged about a problem he has in school or at home, do your best to keep him from sensing how you feel. Talk to someone who can help you figure out ways to support your child. You might talk to your spouse, a close friend, your child's teacher, a social worker, someone at your place of worship, or a counselor.

Remember that your child needs you.
You need to be there for her—nothing in the world can replace a parent's love and encouragement.

Setting Goals

Let's look ahead

Q. *How can I help my child set realistic goals—and reach them?*

A. Learning to set goals is an important step on the road to becoming more responsible and independent. Start with reachable short-term goals, and move forward from there.

At the start of the school year, help your child set specific goals that can be achieved as the school year progresses. Let goals combine what excites your child most with what needs improvement. Does your daughter love astronomy but struggle with reading? She could set a goal of reading one interesting book on astronomy each week, or every two weeks. Maybe your son wants to raise his math grade this year. He could set a goal of doing five extra-practice problems each day.

Report-card time is a good time to set goals. Offer positive solutions to the situations that kept your child from reaching a goal. You might ask, "What do you think you can do to improve your spelling grade? Would it help to write your words in the morning when you're fresh?" Also ask what you can do to help your child reach a goal.

Break long-range goals down into smaller goals. For example, to finish a book in a single week, your child could set a goal of reading one chapter each weekday and two chapters on Saturday and Sunday. This will give your child the satisfaction of making tangible progress a day at a time and demonstrate that a big goal doesn't have to be overwhelming.

Have your child write down goals and put them on the refrigerator, on a bedroom mirror, or on a bulletin board over the study table. This will keep your child from losing sight of them.

Michaela's Goals This Quarter
1. Place in the school spelling contest
2. Blue ribbon at the science fair

Michaela's Goals This Week
1. Drill on old spelling words (chapters 1—10), 2 chapters per night
   Memorize new words (chapter 11)
2. Collect at least 20 different rock samples
   Identify types of rocks

Daily reminders help all of us reach goals. It's a good idea to remind kids of their goals and check to see if progress is being made toward reaching them.

It feels great to accomplish a goal! Let your child know that reaching goals—both small ones and large ones—is cause for celebration. To mark the achievement, you might put a certificate of success on the refrigerator, bake a cake together, or have your child invite a friend over for popcorn and a movie.

Talk about the academic growth you've seen in your child throughout the school year. Ask, "What did you do to improve that grade?" "What do you think you're best at in school? Why?" Help your child find ways to use the skills that have helped in some areas to improve in others. You might say, "Studying math facts every night has helped you do well on tests. Maybe your vocabulary quizzes would go better if you made up some sentences for them every day."

Look together at the end-of-the-year report card. What's gone well? Where does your child need help? Use a long break as a time to work on areas needing improvement. Seek tutoring, ask the teacher for resources, use the library, or go to a good children's bookstore or school supply store to find materials to help your child improve skills.

Help your child learn about the broad range of jobs and careers. Talk about the work you do and how you came to do it. You might be a carpenter, a homemaker, an airline pilot, a dog-sitter, a lawyer, a computer programmer, a student, a childcare worker, a sculptor, a cook, a teacher, an office manager, a salesperson . . . or something else. Did you know what you wanted to do when you were younger? How did you know or find out? Where did you learn the skills you needed? How did you decide where to go to school? What are your future career goals? Sharing this information will get your child thinking about future options.

If you work outside the home, take your child to work with you for the day. If you work nights, you might be able to arrange a brief daytime visit. Seeing where you work will present a new view of you and expand your child's understanding of the world of work. For many kids, knowing what a parent does at work can also be comforting. It lets them picture what Dad or Mom is doing while away from home.

As you travel around your community or farther away, point out universities, community colleges, technical schools, military bases, art or drama schools, and other places that prepare people for careers. Seeing these places will help kids visualize themselves in one of them. Talk about why people choose to go to particular schools and how this helps them progress toward their future goals. ("There's the school where disc jockeys learn about working on the radio. What do you suppose they have to learn?" "That's a teaching hospital. People learn to be doctors and nurses there.") Also talk about the kind of school your child might choose after high school.

FYI

To get your child thinking about careers, check out these books from the "Career Ideas for Kids" series. The books include activities and exercises to help kids rate their interests and aptitudes in different areas and learn how to prepare for careers that interest them—careers like animator, archaeologist, broadcaster, clergy person, fitness instructor, floral designer, oceanographer, and photojournalist. Book sections include "Get in Gear," "Take a Trip," "Don't Stop Now," and "Future Destinations"; each volume profiles fifteen different careers.

Career Ideas for Kids Who Like Art and *Career Ideas for Kids Who Like Science* by Diane Lindsey Reeves (New York: Facts on File, 1998).

Career Ideas for Kids Who Like Sports by Diane Lindsey Reeves and Nancy Bond (New York: Checkmark Books, 1998).

Career Ideas for Kids Who Like Talking by Diane Lindsey Reeves and Nancy Heubeck (New York: Facts on File, 1998).

Enrichment

Learning from life

Q. *What can I do to encourage learning when my child isn't busy with schoolwork?*

A. There are many ways to make learning part of everyday life. Each experience broadens a child's knowledge base and understanding of the world and how it works.

Teach your child to appreciate differences among people. Also help your child understand how much people have in common: "The hat the man's wearing is called a turban. I think he's wearing it because of his religion—just like Uncle Saul wears a yarmulke. Maybe we can find out more about it at the library."

Take advantage of "teachable moments" when your child sees or asks about differences. For example, in response to a question about a child in a wheelchair you might say, "You're right—the girl's in a wheelchair. People use wheelchairs when they aren't able to walk on their own. Wheelchairs make it possible for them to get around. Did you know that some people race their wheelchairs, like you run races with your brother?"

Visit different parts of your community and state or province. If you live in the city, visit a farm or farm museum. If you live in the suburbs, go into the city and take your own walking tour. Actually seeing the differences among urban, suburban, small-town, and rural settings helps your child understand how ways of life are different and similar.

Regional festivals highlight various cultures. Take advantage of these for a fun and educational family outing. The possibilities will vary depending on where you live. How about going to a St. Patrick's Day parade, a Native American powwow, a Mexican market, or a Lithuanian dance exhibition? The library might feature traditional storytelling from Africa, Japan, Russia, or Latin America. Sample piroshki, egg rolls, or barbecue at an ethnic food festival. Go to museums and art shows to explore local arts-and-crafts traditions such as quilts, tapestries, beadwork, pottery, or wood and stone carvings. Check the newspaper or regional magazines to find these kinds of activities.

Teach your child patriotic songs such as "The Star-Spangled Banner," "O Canada," or "Advance Australia Fair." There are many occasions at school (and other events) when kids have a chance to sing the national anthem. A child who knows the words can sing along with gusto! Talk with your child about why most nations have their own patriotic music and what can be positive and negative about patriotic pride.

Notice and talk about flags. Why do people display flags? What does a flag stand for? Why do people sometimes burn flags, or treat them in disrespectful ways? Look in an atlas at the flags of the world. Maybe your child would like to create her own flag, or one that represents your family.

Fill your home with books and magazines that will open windows for your child to learn about Earth's peoples and cultures. Even if your child is too young to understand the text of an article, the illustrations can lead to rich discussions about how people live in different parts of the community, the country, and the world.

FYI

Here are resources to help your child discover and explore different cultures:

A Child's Celebration of the World (Music for Little People, Warner Brothers Records, 1998). Older and younger kids will enjoy the multicultural songs performed by a variety of musicians. Check your local children's book or toy store or write to Music for Little People, P.O. Box 1460, Redway, CA 95560-1460. Toll-free phone: 1-800-346-4445. Email: *musicforlittlepeople@mflp.com*

The Kingfisher Young People's Atlas of the World by Philip Steele (New York: Kingfisher, 1997). A good resource that introduces lands, peoples, and customs from around the globe.

People by Peter Spier (New York: Double-day, 1988). A wonderful introduction for younger kids to the ways that people are alike and different.

Traditions Around the World: Games by Godfrey Hall (New York: Thomson Learning, 1995). Describes and gives the rules for many of the world's most popular games.

Introduce your child to the daily or weekly newspaper. Start with a section that will spark curiosity—depending on your child's interests, this might be the comics, a world news page, TV or movie listings, a special-interest column, the sports or variety section, or a page written by young people. Point out pictures and articles that your child may want to know about. If you need to check the weather forecast or see what movie is playing, ask your child to look it up in the newspaper.

Discuss current events and how they relate to the past. For example, if farm problems are in the news, share information about small family farms of long ago. Visit a family farm or a large industrial farm. Talk about how farming has changed and why. Shop at a farmers' market and a supermarket and compare the two experiences. Together, talk about what's good and bad about the changes in farming and in the way food is distributed.

Take your child with you when you vote. Showing children how the voting process works is an early lesson in democracy. Talk about who you're voting for and why. Don't be surprised if your child has formed an opinion about a political race. Listen to these ideas, even if you don't agree. This is a great model of respect, and it helps your child understand the value of each individual person's beliefs.

Are you basketball fans? Mix a little geography into the enjoyment of sports. Study the NCAA tournament brackets with your child. Discuss the universities listed and the different regions of the country where they're located.

Share in the fun and discovery of planting and tending something together. You might plant a potted cactus or an herb garden, create a floral patio display, or grow vegetables in your yard or in a community plot. (Kids may be more willing to try different veggies if they've helped raise them.) Find a book on caring for your plants, and work together to nurture them. Besides getting a hands-on lesson in how things grow, your child may also discover (or rediscover) the joy of dirt under the fingernails.

Teach your child that things we throw away end up in landfills. Explain why it's important to conserve paper, water, and energy. Together, plan ways to limit the number of cans and bottles you use. Talk about why you recycle and about where all those newspapers, plastic bottles, glass jars, and aluminum cans go after the truck hauls them away. The more practical information kids have about using and safeguarding the world's natural resources, the more likely they are to look for ways to conserve them.

Enjoy the outdoors together—it's a terrific classroom. Hiking forest trails and mountain paths gives kids firsthand understanding of some of the land forms they're learning about in school.

Put on old sneakers and go for a walk together in a creek. Take along a pocket guide on birds and animals. Turn over a few rocks to see what's underneath. Look at the tracks, feathers, and droppings along the shoreline. Try to figure out what creatures left them.

Make the park or forest come alive for your child by working together to identify trees and other plants by their leaves, stems, bark, and flowers. Keep a log that tells what you discovered and when you saw it. Add to the log on each outdoor adventure.

Choose a clear night to take a blanket outside and stargaze. Lie back and enjoy the wonders of the night sky. See what constellations and planets you can name.

Take along a ditch-digging shovel to the beach. This sturdy, short-handled shovel is easy for even a young child to use, which makes it a great tool for playing and building in the sand. You can find one at an army surplus or home-and-garden store.

Dig and build in the sand with your child. Let yourselves be engineers who test different building techniques. Encourage your child to ask questions and figure out solutions: "How do I keep this trench from filling with water?" "What can I do to keep the tide from washing away my wall?" "Will the sand from deeper in the ground be any firmer than the sand on top?"

Take your child berry picking—it's "berry" fun! And it's a great way to discover how strawberries or blueberries are grown and harvested.

Go camping with your child. Cook over a campfire, read or play games by the light of a lantern, and sleep in a tent. Enjoy the simple pleasures of "keeping house" in the out-of-doors. Talk about how people used to live before the days of electricity, running water, and grocery stores.

Start a family bird-watching diary. Place a birdfeeder where you can watch it from inside your home. Buy a book on birds and get your child involved in feeding and identifying the birds that come to visit. Keep a small notebook and pen near the window so that you and your child can write down and date the sightings of different birds. Over time, you'll be able to compare the habits of birds from season to season and year to year.

Whether you have a home computer or not, chances are your child is using a computer at school and in friends' homes. If you have a computer, sit down at it with your child. Play games together, or use a publishing or word-processing program to make cards or banners. If you don't have this technology at home, use a computer and software at your local library.

Join your child in cyberspace and surf the Net together. (If you're clueless about how to do this, ask your child—who may have lots to teach you about navigating the World Wide Web.) Is your son or daughter computer-savvy? Ask your child to show you favorite Web sites and chat rooms. Or go exploring together. Computers offer a great opportunity for parents and kids to have fun and learn together.

FYI

Some computer games are just for fun while others enrich learning, too. Here's a resource you can check to find some of the better games on the market:

Oppenheim Toy Portfolio, 1999: The Best Toys, Books, Videos, Music & Software for Kids (6th Edition) by Joanne F. Oppenheim, Stephanie Oppenheim, and James Oppenheim (New York: Oppenheim, 1998). Oppenheim Toy Portfolio is a nationally recognized consumer organization, and this book is updated annually.

Get your child involved in craft activities from kits or magazines. Crafts give kids experience in reading and following directions and let them create wonderful finished products of their own. Children's stores, bookstores, hobby and nature stores, and even yard or tag sales will have books and activity sets. You'll also find kits to buy over the Internet. Your child might make a book, create notecards, set up a display for a collection, or build a model airplane. These are also great projects the two of you can do together.

Do you have a first grader who likes to draw and fingerpaint? Let your younger child practice spelling words or math facts by writing in shaving cream on the kitchen table. It's motivating and fun, and it involves your child by using a variety of learning styles.

Get in the museum habit. Take out a family membership, or visit during free or reduced-price hours. Many museums include interactive exhibits and activities especially for children.

Show your child how to do a cross-word puzzle or a word jumble in the newspaper. If you like, do the daily or weekly crossword together.

Encourage an older child to read aloud to a younger one. This gives the big sister or brother a chance to teach and lead, and gives the younger child a fantastic role model. (It might offer you a few minutes of relaxation, too!) Kids often enjoy sharing a magazine. Check out the library's collection. Maybe there's one your child would like to subscribe to or check out each month.

FYI

There are dozens of magazines for kids in a variety of interest areas. Here are a few of our favorites:

Cobblestone and *Footsteps*. *Cobblestone* is a U.S. history magazine; *Footsteps* features articles with African-American heritage themes. Write to Cobblestone Publishing, 30 Grove Street, Suite C, Peterborough, NH 03458. Phone number: (603) 924-7209.

Cricket and *Spider*. Stories, science fiction, biographies, sports, travel, animals, poems, and humor for young readers. *Cricket* is for ages 9 and up. *Spider* is for ages 6–9. Write to Cricket Magazine Group, 112 Tenth Street, Des Moines, IA 50309. Toll-free phone: 1-800-827-0227. Web address: *http://www.cricketmag.com*

National Geographic World. Makes geography and sociology exciting for readers ages 8–14. Write to World Magazine, P.O. Box 63001, Tampa, FL 33663-3001. Toll-free phone: 1-800-647-5463. Web address: *http://www.nationalgeographic.com/world*

If you clip and save grocery coupons, ask your child to sort them by type and to discard the expired ones. You'll be reinforcing two basic math concepts: sorting (classifying) and understanding how a calendar works.

Make a meal or bake cookies together. Measuring sugar and figuring out how to double a recipe reinforce math skills. Learning when to grease the pan and how baking soda or egg whites help cakes rise teaches science concepts. Cooking is often a fun learning experience even for young children. Let your child be creative in decorating or serving the food.

Is your child learning to figure percentages? If so, enlist his help when you shop or eat out. Ask your child to calculate the tip in a restaurant, the tax on something you want to buy, or the price of an item that's 20 percent off.

Get your child involved in music. Music teaches self-discipline and team-work and supports math learning. (It's also lively, hands-on fun.) If the school has a band program, encourage your child to join. Ask the music teacher about renting or purchasing a second-hand instrument. Enroll your child in music lessons, a choir, or a community dance program. Ask around about a good instructor. The right teacher can bring out the best in students.

Encourage your child to listen to different types of music—anything from hip-hop to polkas to madrigals to reggae. Play tapes, CDs, or a variety of radio stations while doing chores or fixing meals. Sing and dance along!

Movies and TV shows will expose your child to all types of people. Point out stereotyping or discrimination in the media. Talk about where stereotypes come from and why they can both help and hurt our understanding of other people.

Set rules about the TV and computer.
What programs, movies, and music
videos do you want your child to watch?
What games do you want her to play?
What Web sites do you want her to visit?
If your child has a favorite program or
chat room you're not familiar with,
check it out. Also set rules for how much
time your child will spend with the TV
and computer each day. A good rule
is no more than two hours—though less
is better. Talk with your child about
the rules, and be willing to negotiate in
special circumstances.

Listening is a skill all kids need to develop. Play listening games like Telephone, Going on a Trip ("I'm going on a trip and I'm taking along . . ."), and Twenty Questions with your child. They're great for passing the time on rides across town or cross-country.

Play card games, board games, memory games, trivia games, and other games that require thinking skills. There are literally hundreds of these that you and your child can enjoy together. Games let kids practice important skills like adding, subtracting, making change, and thinking logically and creatively.

Ask questions that require your child to think things through before answering. Instead of asking "Did you have fun?" ask "Why was that so much fun?" Here are a few good question starters: "Suppose," "I wonder whether," "How," and "What if . . . ?"

Personal
Responsibility

Moving toward independence

Q. *How can I encourage my child to be both cooperative and independent?*

A. This can be a tricky balance. The secret is to provide structure and limits along with freedom and responsibility.

Teach and model self-control. In school, kids need to be able to stay in their seats, listen, and wait their turn to talk. It's easier for children to do these things in the classroom if they get plenty of practice doing them at home. Use mealtime as an opportunity to encourage patience and self-control. Remind everyone in the family not to interrupt people's phone conversations. Tell your child what you expect, and show it by your own actions, too.

Kids need to work quietly on their own some of the time. At home, establish a set quiet time or "no-noise hour" for studying and reading. Encourage your child to work independently without asking for help during the first fifteen or twenty minutes on a homework assignment.

Help your child accept and cope with disappointment. One way to do this is by making it a point to show how *you* deal with it. You might say, "I'm very disappointed that I didn't get the job I wanted. I guess I'll have to keep trying." Guide your child to express her own disappointment, too: "You wish you could go to the movie. I know you're disappointed. But it's not okay to yell at me. Would you like to talk about ideas for what you can do instead?"

Set clear rules and limits in your home. Explain them to your child firmly and respectfully: "I know you want to play action games some more. But we need it quiet after supper so you and your sister can study. You can play some more this weekend."

Kids thrive under structure, so stick to the limits you set. Your child won't have to beg you to change your mind if "No" means "No" in your home.

When it's possible, offer choices: "You can either play a game or go to the park with Jill. You decide." "Would you rather help me with the dishes now, or in an hour?" Children need the chance to make choices so that they learn to be responsible for their own decisions. The choices will vary, depending on your child's age and maturity.

Give your child responsibilities at home. Allow some give-and-take in choosing chores and setting timelines. Don't be surprised if you have to do a little reminding, but do expect your child to complete chores.

Set reasonable standards for how home chores are to be done. Then put the standards in writing so there won't be any misunderstandings or confusion. You might find it helpful to have your child sign an agreement. Keep the written agreement on a kitchen bulletin board, on the refrigerator, or in some other handy place.

Break chores down into simple steps. This helps your child learn how to manage a job that may otherwise seem overwhelming. And it can keep you from having to follow behind him reminding or redoing tasks.

Kitchen Cleanup

1. Rinse dishes.
2. Load them into dishwasher.
3. Wipe stove, counters, and table.
4. Sweep floor.

Give your child an alarm clock. Kids need to rise to meet their responsibilities, and having an alarm clock of their own can help them do that. It can also help parents avoid struggles with a sleepyhead.

Fables and folktales teach the lessons of life. Read fairy tales, folk stories, and fables to your child. Talk about what people can learn from them.

FYI

Here's a book of folktales you and your child might enjoy:

Favorite Folktales from Around the World edited by Jane Yolen (New York: Pantheon Books, 1988). A wonderful collection of the world's best folktales, chosen by an internationally known storyteller.

Talk to the parents of your child's friends. Find out what their family rules are for using the TV, computer, or phone. Knowing these things can help you make decisions about the time your child spends in friends' homes. At the same time, when other children visit your home, teach your child to respect their family rules. Don't "loosen up" the rules for someone else's child, even if you think the parent is too strict.

Take care in choosing TV shows and movies you watch when your child is present. Many kids aren't mature enough to watch things that are acceptable for adults. For example, you (and the teacher) probably won't be happy to hear your child repeat off-color jokes from an adult comedy hour. Or, a child may seem to enjoy a horror movie but then have nightmares several days later. TV and the Internet make all kinds of material easily available to kids. This means parents have to be extra-vigilant in screening what their children view.

FYI

For help with screening what your child views on the Internet, you may want to check out Mayberry, U.S.A., an Internet screening service that blocks or filters pornography, hate groups, and other objectionable material. Toll-free phone: 1-800-383-5854. Web address: *http://www.mbusa.net*

On the Web, visit "Unglued from the Tube," where critic Diana Dawson previews television shows and makes recommendations for parents. At the Web site, click onto "TV news" and then click onto "Unglued from the Tube." Web address: *http://www.clicktv.com*

Listen to the music your child likes.
Do you think it's appropriate? If you don't like what you hear, tell your child. Explain why you're putting that music off limits. Suggest alternatives.

Make it a policy that no child is to visit your home when there's not an adult home to supervise. Tell your child that the same rule applies when she is a guest in another child's home.

Don't accept "But everybody else's parents let them do it." That's often not how it really is! Talk to other parents to learn firsthand their rules about overnights, bedtime, and weekend activities.

Guide your child to stick to agreements. Once your child has decided to join the ball team, the band, or the computer club at school, help him hold to the commitment. Don't be in a hurry to let him quit if the going gets rough. Explain that it's important for people to follow through and do what they've agreed to. Hanging in there teaches "stick-to-it-iveness." And a child who knows quitting isn't an option is likely to make future decisions more carefully.

Good sports etiquette carries over into the classroom. When you're watching or participating in a game, keep your cheering friendly, and don't yell at the coaches or boo the other team, even in fun. A child who knows that Dad or Mom doesn't think the referees and coaches are being fair could start to lose the sporting spirit.

Help your child to be a good loser by not putting too much emphasis on winning. This goes for academic competitions as well as sports.

FYI

Libraries have books and videos about how children develop and what you can expect at different ages. Here are three helpful books:

The Parent's Handbook: Systematic Training for Effective Parenting (STEP) by Don Dinkmeyer, Gary D. McKay, and Don Dinkmeyer, Jr. (Circle Pines, MN: American Guidance Service, 1997). A basic resource on encouraging good behavior, setting limits, and building independence. Includes real-life examples.

How to Handle a Hard-to-Handle Kid: A Parents' Guide to Understanding and Changing Problem Behaviors by C. Drew Edwards, Ph.D. (Minneapolis: Free Spirit Publishing, 1999). Some children argue, disobey, and throw temper tantrums more often than others. This book is full of ideas for turning the problem around.

The Explosive Child: A New Approach for Understanding and Parenting Easily Frustrated "Chronically Inflexible" Children by Ross W. Greene, Ph.D. (New York: HarperCollins, 1998). Discusses the origins of children's "meltdowns" and presents strategies to help prevent them.

Get the facts when your child is disciplined for misbehaving at school.
Kids need to understand that there are consequences for their actions. Sometimes children don't want to admit that they've done something wrong. At other times, they feel unfairly singled out. For example, a child may admit she was throwing food in the lunchroom but claim she was just one of many. In situations like this, help your child think about her own actions.

There might be a time when your child has been disciplined along with the whole class for something he did not do. The teacher may have had a reason for disciplining the entire group. Ask the teacher about what happened. This will help you understand her point of view and may also help you talk about the situation with your child.

Talk to the teacher privately if you feel your child has not been treated fairly. Let the teacher know your point of view, and listen to his as well. At the same time, be realistic in your expectations of your child's teacher. While he is very concerned about your child, he must also think about what's best for the group.

Encourage your child to lend a helping hand. Even young children have something to offer others. Your child could carry someone's groceries, help a neighbor rake leaves, or assist in caring for a pet. Pitch in yourself sometimes, too. Children who are helpful at home and in their neighborhoods bring an important skill to school with them and often become models for the other kids. Kindness is contagious!

You are your child's first and most important teacher. Everything you do to teach the values that are important to you will help your child along the path to independence and responsibility.

Getting Along
with Others

It's all about respect

Q. *Sometimes the world seems unfair and unkind. How can I help my child find positive ways to get along with friends and teachers?*

A. Emphasize the Golden Rule: "Treat others the way you want to be treated." It will help your child learn and remember to treat others with respect, even when there's a problem.

Respect is the key to getting along with others. A child who knows how it feels to be respected can learn to treat other people with respect. You show respect by listening when your child talks to you and by letting her know that you care about the things that please— and worry—her. You also show it when you *don't* do things for your child that she's capable of doing for herself.

Emphasize good manners. Teach your child that "Please," "Thank you," and "Excuse me" are words that show respect and help people get along. Encourage your child to make eye contact when speaking with someone. Remind your son or daughter to listen and speak politely to teachers and other people.

PLEASE

THANK YOU!

EXCUSE ME

Teach your child how to make introductions. Demonstrate how to smile and say hello, tell your name, ask the other person's name, shake hands, and say "It's nice to meet you." Also teach your child to introduce one person to another.

Help everyone in your home feel comfortable saying (and meaning) "I'm sorry." Many kids understand the reason for an apology when they've done something wrong or unkind on purpose. ("I'm sorry I borrowed your book without asking. I'll be sure to ask you next time." "I'm sorry I used up the last of the red paper instead of sharing it.") But children sometimes think there's no reason to apologize when their action was a mistake or an accident. In school, we want kids to know both that mistakes are okay and that it's important to say "I'm sorry" if a mistake has hurt someone else. For example, Lucy may swing her feet in her chair and accidentally kick Tyrone. Tyrone may not know that Lucy wasn't kicking on purpose. If Lucy doesn't apologize, Tyrone may get angry. There could be a conflict when a simple "I'm sorry" could have cleared everything up.

I'M SORRY.

Encourage your daughter or son to get in the habit of writing thank-you notes. Your child will be practicing good manners and developing writing skills at the same time.

Dear Luis,

Thank you for the yo-yo you gave me for my birthday. I really like it!

Your friend,

Marya

Talk about phone etiquette. In this age of call waiting, caller ID, and voice mail, simple courtesy is sometimes forgotten. As a family, talk through rules for everyone to follow when answering and using the phone. Besides making home life smoother, this will help your child understand some of the practical reasons for common courtesy.

Chaperone a class field trip or another large-group outing. Observe how kids talk and act. Afterward, talk to your child about what you saw. Compliment good behavior and point out both nice and not-so-nice things you noticed taking place. Use your chat as an opportunity to reinforce good manners.

Help your child respect authority. Guide her through situations where she must deal with teachers, leaders, and other authority figures. Help her learn how to approach these people with respect when there are problems. For example, suppose your daughter was disciplined for talking with several other kids during a test. She's upset because she wasn't talking, but was sitting in the middle of a group of kids who were. You can talk with her about steps to follow to resolve the problem between her and the teacher. You can tell your child to follow these guidelines:

1. Ask the teacher for a time to talk privately together.
2. Calmly tell her side of the story to the teacher.
3. Listen respectfully to what the teacher has to say.
4. Respond with respect even if she doesn't agree with the teacher.
5. Talk to you about what to do next if the situation isn't resolved.

Little feelings get hurt in a big way when invitations are passed out at school. Remind your child not to talk about a party in front of people who aren't included. Send party invitations through the mail or deliver them to children's homes in person.

Help your child learn to share. This may sound obvious, but many kids don't fully understand that in school they need to share books, games, computers and other equipment, art materials, and the teacher's time. At home, start with sharing toys and treats. Progress to sharing work and responsibility.

Teach your child to accept and appreciate different people. If your child hears or makes an unkind remark about someone from another race or culture, talk about it. Explain the word *prejudice* — a strong feeling of like or dislike that isn't based on reason. Teach your child that prejudice comes from a lack of knowledge about someone and a lack of respect. Help your son or daughter find ways to learn about others, and welcome people from different backgrounds to your home.

Never let your child use negative words or gestures to refer to a person with a disability. Don't allow kids in your home to call someone a "retard" or describe a person as "crippled." Teach your child respectful, matter-of-fact words: "a boy who has Down syndrome," "a girl who is hard of hearing," "a woman who is paralyzed." Help your child understand that all people are valuable. Each of us can do some things and can't do others. We all have feelings that can be hurt. We all deserve courtesy and respect.

Some things are for adult ears only. Swearing and discussions or criticisms about others may be repeated at school, so be careful what you say around a child.

Model warmth toward others. Your child will learn from your example.

Welcome your child's friends to your home. Encourage your child to reach out to make new ones, too. It's important for kids to take some of the responsibility for making and keeping friends. Rather than waiting for others to make the first move, prompt your child to invite a classmate over. Suggest some things the two of them might do together.

Take care not to leave others with hurt feelings when your child has special plans to bring a friend home from school. For example, you might suggest, "Why not call Amanda to see if she wants to come home with you after school tomorrow? Let's make all the arrangements by phone. Then you won't have to talk about it in school, and your other friends won't feel left out."

Arrange for back-and-forth visits between homes. Maybe your child feels more comfortable inviting a friend to your home than going to an unfamiliar place. Or maybe the opposite is true, and the friend's home seems more exciting. You can help your child build basic social skills by finding ways to spend time at each home.

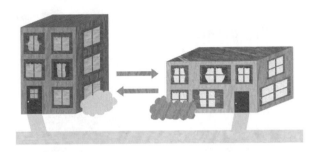

If your child feels uncomfortable in a particular home, don't pressure him to visit there. Listen to his concerns and try to find out why the home doesn't feel safe and welcoming for your child.

Help your child get the most from a "mainstreamed" classroom. Your child might be in a regular classroom that includes kids with special needs. Or maybe your child or other children in the class have special talents or learning differences. Welcome this as an opportunity for your child to learn about, help, and be helped by others. Kids learn compassion, acceptance, and understanding when they work together with people of different needs and abilities. If the class has a buddy program that teams kids who can support each other, encourage your child to participate. You might even suggest such a program to the teacher. (See page 101 for some resources on learning differences.)

Try to get the whole story about a problem at school. Often a child's view of things is incomplete or one-sided. Keep this in mind when listening to what your child tells you. Talk to the teacher or to other parents to learn as much as you can about what has happened.

Let your child see you and the teacher working together as a team. When your child is having a conflict in the classroom, resist the urge to criticize or blame someone. Talk with the teacher to learn all about the problem. There may be important details that you aren't aware of. It's also possible that the teacher doesn't know how a situation is affecting your child.

Give your child a chance to express feelings. Children are sometimes harsh critics of others. When they're hurt or angry, don't take everything they say about a friend to heart. Sometimes a child just needs to vent some strong feelings. If you keep noticing the same kinds of upset feelings over and over, it's time to dig a little deeper.

Teach your child how to use "I-statements" to talk about feelings with others. I-statements let a child express feelings clearly and firmly but without blaming anyone: "I don't like it when you push ahead of me in line. I wish you would wait your turn." "When you go in my desk and take my pencils, I get mad. Please ask me first."

Model a calm, thoughtful approach to solving a conflict. Start by listening respectfully and acknowledging your child's feelings. Resist getting emotionally charged about the situation yourself. Ask your child questions to help her understand the problem and find ways to resolve it: "I can tell that you're really angry about what happened. Why do you think Josh did that? What could you say to him so he won't do it again?"

When the two of you have a conflict, make sure your child takes some of the responsibility for resolving it. Teach your child these problem-solving steps:

1. Say what the problem is.
2. Tell what happened and how each person feels about it.
3. Come up with ideas for solving the problem. Think about what might happen for each idea, and then choose the best idea to try first.
4. Try out your idea.
5. Look at how the idea worked and decide what to do next.

Help your child role-play ways to deal with a dilemma at school. Talk together about a problem that's happening. Then act out the situation to help your child find ways to handle it. This will help your daughter or son feel ready and confident to deal with school problems in a constructive way.

Some problems, such as being bullied, are too big for kids to handle alone. A child who is being hurt by other kids needs to know that it's okay—and it's not tattling—to talk to an adult. In these cases, don't hesitate to contact the school. The teacher might not be aware of the situation. At the same time, talk with your child about what to do when bullying happens. You might want to role-play things your child can say or do when confronted by a bully.

—— FYI ——

Here are books to help kids learn to solve conflicts and deal with bullying:

We Can Get Along: A Child's Book of Choices by Lauren Murphy Payne, M.S.W., and Claudia Rohling, M.S.W. (Minneapolis: Free Spirit Publishing, 1997). Teaches essential peacemaking skills in a way children ages 5–8 will understand.

What to Do . . . When Kids Are Mean to Your Child: Real Solutions from Experts, Parents, and Kids by Elin McCoy (Pleasantville, NY: Reader's Digest, 1997). Includes real-life vignettes, "quick reference" strategies, and resources. For parents of kids ages 5–13.

Bullies Are a Pain in the Brain by Trevor Romain (Minneapolis: Free Spirit Publishing, 1997). Blends humor with sound ideas for becoming "Bully-Proof."

What Do You Think? A Kid's Guide to Dealing with Daily Dilemmas by Linda Schwartz, illustrated by Beverly Armstrong (Santa Barbara, CA: The Learning Works, 1993). Helps kids look at issues from different points of view. Ages 8–12.

Teach your child that violence is not okay. Make sure your son or daughter knows that fighting, hitting, name calling, and threatening are not acceptable ways to solve problems. Help your child understand feelings of anger and frustration. Suggest some nonviolent ways to express them, such as running around the block, punching a pillow, or writing about the feelings.

If you see that your child can't seem to get rid of angry feelings, seek help. Be alert to disturbing behavior, too. For example, excessive bullying or fighting, setting fires, being cruel to animals, or a lack of friends can all signal serious problems. Talk to the school counselor or social worker or with a professional at a mental health center.

When your child is worried about a friend, listen. Your daughter or son may tell you that another child is threatening others, being violent, using drugs, or feeling depressed. Share this information with the child's parent or with a professional you trust, such as the teacher or the school's student assistance counselor, psychologist, or principal.

Volunteering

We're all in this together

Q. *I want to be a part of my child's school. What are some ways I can get involved?*

A. Schools need parents' help—both their brain power and their muscle power. Start by calling the school to find out where help is most needed.

Most teachers welcome a parent's helping hand in the classroom. Teachers need help with a variety of tasks. Making bulletin boards, grading papers, photocopying materials, tutoring students, and assisting with art projects are just a few of the ways you might pitch in.

Many employers support parent participation in school activities. Some states have laws that require employers to allow workers time off to attend certain school functions. Beyond that, the provisions vary from company to company. Check out the offerings and procedures where you work. Do what you can to support workplace policies that are school- and family-friendly.

It's usually most effective for volunteers to have a regularly scheduled day or time period for volunteering. Work with the teacher to set up a routine for helping in school. This way the teacher can have work ready for you to do before you arrive.

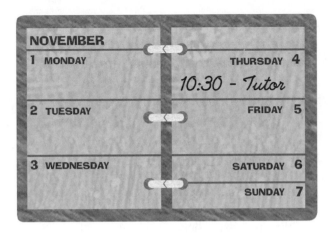

Arrive on time and be ready to do what the teacher asks of you. If you feel you need clearer direction or training, ask for it. The teacher may want to meet with you before or after school to go over some of your tasks. Or, she may ask you to take some orientation offered through the school or through community education.

Grandparents can be a great resource to schools. As kids get older and busier, their relationships with grandparents can sometimes lose ground. If your child's grandparents live nearby, talk to them about helping at school. When a grandparent who lives elsewhere comes to visit, arrange a visit to school for lunch. This helps Grandma or Grandpa see your child's school life firsthand.

Volunteer to talk to the class about your job or special interest. Elementary school students love visitors. Middle school teachers appreciate parent speakers or demonstrations, too. Could you teach the family-living class how to make potato latkes? Share your scuba diving slides with a science class? Maybe you know someone else who would make a great classroom guest.

Do you have a cultural tradition to share with your child's class? If so, contact the teacher to schedule a visit to the class. Many teachers are on the lookout for this type of learning experience for their students.

Let your child know that when you volunteer at school you are there to help the teacher. Explain that you can't give your child special attention during this time. If your daughter or son gets embarrassed or acts silly, you could check about volunteering for a different teacher.

While volunteering at school, you may inadvertently overhear personal remarks or see private records concerning a child. Take special care to respect a child's privacy and keep this information confidential.

You can make a big difference by getting involved in policy-setting organizations. For example, you might ask to be appointed to a curriculum review committee or to work on a school-based initiative concerned with violence prevention. Contact the district office, the volunteer coordinator, or the school office to learn how you can help.

Join the Parent Teacher Association (PTA) or Parent Teacher Student Organization (PTSO) at your school. Better yet, volunteer to help out with PTA- or PTSO-sponsored events. If you can spare the time, take on the job of being an officer in the organization. You may even want to seek an appointment as a member of your school board. These are all organizations that offer you a chance to have a real impact on your child's school.

Find out what plans your PTA or PTSO has to honor the staff during Teacher Appreciation Week. Do what you can to help. This kind of recognition means a lot to teachers.

FYI

In the U.S., increasing parent involvement has become an objective of state and federal government. Your PTA or PTSO might want to order this report:

Playing Their Parts: Parents and Teachers Talk About Parental Involvement in the Public Schools by Steve Farkas, Jean Johnson, and Ann Duffett with Claire Aulicino and Joanna McHugh (New York: Public Agenda, 1999). Summarizes findings from national surveys on how parents are and should be involved in school and what issues concern both teachers and parents. Write to Public Agenda, 6 East 39th Street, New York, NY 10016, or call (212) 686-6610. Web address: *http://www.publicagenda.org*

Volunteer your labor for schoolyard projects. You might help with building an outdoor activity center, repairing playground equipment, or landscaping around the building. Take your child along when you work. It's good for her to see you working on a community project. And it shows her how important her school is to you.

Help with school events like carnivals or music programs. These activities present opportunities for parents to participate in the way that's best suited to them. For example, you might make phone calls, create or decorate placards, handle sign-ups for staffing booths, sell tickets, arrange for refreshments, or serve as the treasurer.

See if your employer can donate something for a school fund-raiser. Maybe your company could provide drinking cups, paper or printing for fliers, or prizes. Businesses get tax breaks for making these donations, and many companies welcome the chance to contribute to the school and community.

If you sign up for a task and find you can't make it, let the appropriate person know in plenty of time to make other arrangements.

When school personnel notice the talents of a good volunteer, all types of projects come to mind. Any help you can offer will be appreciated, but don't feel obligated to take on more than you can comfortably handle.

Old magazines serve a multitude of purposes in a classroom. Before you send yours off for recycling, call the teacher, art specialist, librarian, or media director to see if the school could use them.

Tell your child about volunteer work you do outside of school. Maybe you give blood, collect money for a foundation, handle the phones for a public television drive, visit residents at a health-care center, or volunteer at a shelter. Talk to your child about why you give your time in this way. Describe how good it feels to help. If possible, bring your child along some of the time.

Support *service learning* in your child's school. Many schools have requirements or opportunities for kids to spend volunteer hours in the community. Encourage your son or daughter to take part in these activities. Kids sometimes need help choosing situations that fit their interests. If service learning isn't part of your child's school program, talk to the teacher or principal about getting it started.

Holidays and Breaks

Making the most of them

Q. *Sometimes it seems that there are as many "special" days and days off as there are regular school days. How can I make the most of these changes in the routine?*

A. Holidays and breaks offer lots of learning opportunities. They also give you and your child a chance to enrich your relationship.

Check with the teacher before sending treats or party favors to school. Classrooms generally recognize birthdays with a song or with pencils or stickers, but there are exceptions to this. Some schools, for instance, forego celebrations because of regulations about the use of instructional time. And some districts have dietary and health policies that allow only approved foods to be served.

Let the teacher know if you don't want your child to take part in birthday or other celebrations. In this case, also talk to your child about what to do during these classroom events.

Some children get so excited about birthdays that they have trouble focusing in school. For this reason, it's probably best to save gestures of recognition like balloon bouquets or flowers for the home celebration.

As with birthdays, let the teacher know if you don't want your child to take part in Halloween activities. Knowing in advance lets the teacher plan a different activity for your child without drawing attention to him. Everyone will be more at ease.

Find out the school's policies regarding Halloween. If the school doesn't allow costumes or candy, it's not because officials want to take all the fun away. Talk to the teacher or principal to find out the reasons behind the school's policy.

There's a good chance that your child's class will talk about Halloween safety. Ask the teacher what will be discussed. Then give your child other information to fill in the blanks: "Wear reflective stickers on your clothes." "Go to only those homes you know." "Have Mom or Dad check your candy before you eat it." "Stick together with your group."

Many schools, places of worship, and community centers have family Halloween parties. If there's not one in your community, work with other parents and the school to organize one. A well-planned party can be a fun and safe alternative to trick-or-treating.

On Veteran's Day, tell your child about friends and family who have served their country in the armed forces. Perhaps you have a picture to share. This is a perfect opportunity to make history real for your daughter or son. To honor the day, maybe your child would like to make a poster or card for residents of a local veteran's hospital.

Include your child in planning special holiday meals. This offers a chance for firsthand learning about preparing tasty, healthy food. You might plan a meal together using the Food Guide Pyramid (see page 56). If your child has a favorite dish, be sure to include it.

On Thanksgiving, have your child help with kitchen tasks. A younger child can measure ingredients, mash potatoes, and roll out pie crusts (or take the frozen pies out of the boxes!). An older child might like to fix something from scratch. Besides having a chance to spend time with the family, your child will be honing skills in following directions and carrying out projects.

FYI

Check out these books that can help you and your child learn more about the history of Thanksgiving:

The First Thanksgiving by Jean Craighead George, illustrated by Thomas Locker (New York: PaperStar, 1996). An interesting and beautifully illustrated book that offers a balanced view of the celebration that the Pilgrims called a Harvest Feast and the Indians thought of as a Green Corn Dance.

If You Sailed on the Mayflower in 1620 by Ann McGovern, illustrated by Anna DiVito (New York: Scholastic, 1993). Follow the journey of the Pilgrims from the time they embark from England until they celebrate the first Thanksgiving.

When the class is looking forward to a holiday break, remind your child to keep up the effort in school. Most kids are in the classroom for about 180 days out of the year. It's important that they get the most out of every one of these days. The teacher will truly appreciate your efforts to help your child stay focused!

If your school has a holiday festival, mark your calendar and attend as a family. Events like this promote a good connection between home and school. They're also usually important fund-raisers for the school.

Add some customs from other cultures and traditions to your own family celebrations. Do you want your child to learn about how people in different parts of the world celebrate Christmas? Hanukkah? Kwanzaa? Ramadan? Chinese New Year? Use the library or the Internet to find books about these holidays and more.

If your child's class has a holiday gift exchange, stick to the recommended gift price. Think of it this way: No more, no less—no problems! Talk to the teacher privately if you have concerns about buying and exchanging gifts.

Teach the joy of giving from the heart. Help your child plan or make gifts for another parent, a stepparent, grandparents, sisters and brothers, and friends. A homemade gift might be a simple creation, like a short poem or a pan of brownies. Or it might be more elaborate, like a scrapbook or a completed model. Making any of these gifts will be a great learning experience. And, while making the gift, your child will be thinking about the person who'll receive it.

Let holidays and vacations be a chance for your child to get some quality time with *you*. Keep your expectations for holiday activities manageable. If you don't have a chance to write cards or bake homemade bread, don't fret. The time spent with your family will make the best memories for you and your child.

Teach your child to always thank someone for a gift. Sometimes kids get gifts that they already have or that they don't particularly like. For this situation, you might use role-playing or a little coaching to help your child find a way to say a sincere thank you. ("It's purple— that's my favorite color! Thanks, Grandma.") Remind your child that what counts is the thoughtfulness, and the feelings, of the gift giver.

Try not to say "I'll be glad when the holidays are over." This can be disheartening to a child. Your efforts to stay cheerful will give your child better memories of the holidays.

Over the holidays, leave the gift wrap on the floor and the laundry in the hamper and play with your child. The chores will still be there when you're finished playing.

Make a New Year's resolution to treat yourself as thoughtfully as you treat your loved ones. To really be there for your child, you need to give yourself some time and attention.

If school is closed for Martin Luther King, Jr.'s birthday, plan an activity that focuses on what Dr. King did and stood for. Maybe your library or bookstore will have a reading event to honor this day. Maybe there's a scout breakfast or a community rally.

In honor of Dr. King, teach your child to always pursue a dream. Talk to your child about your own hopes, dreams, and goals. Ask your child to tell you about her dreams, too.

FYI

Share the story of Dr. Martin Luther King's childhood and teachings. Here are three resources we can recommend for Martin Luther King, Jr. Day:

A Picture Book of Martin Luther King, Jr. by David A. Adler, illustrated by Robert Casilla (New York: Holiday House, 1989). Illustrates Dr. King's life and work in a format that's quick to read and that has a broad appeal for elementary and middle school kids.

I Have a Dream: The Story of Martin Luther King by Margaret Davidson (New York: Scholastic, 1986). A chapter book at about a third-grade reading level that offers an in-depth biography of King and how he changed the course of American history.

I Have a Dream by Martin Luther King, Jr. and Coretta Scott King (New York: Scholastic, 1997). Dr. King's famous speech, still timely today, is presented for children and adults of all ages. Includes striking pictures by fifteen illustrators.

In the U.S., February is Black History Month. Take advantage of local plays, concerts, and other events focused on black history. At the library or bookstore, find books and videos that tell the stories of courageous Americans like Harriet Tubman, Frederick Douglass, Rosa Parks, and others.

If the class exchanges valentines, be sure your child writes a card for each person. Request a student list if the teacher doesn't send one home. Give your child plenty of time to sign and write any notes on the cards: let some responsibilities belong to your child alone.

Keep Valentine's Day a happy holiday. If your child has a gift for a special school friend, remind him to exchange it privately, not at school. This way no one's feelings will be hurt.

On Presidents' Day, tell your child about the president you most admire. You never know—perhaps your son or daughter will be sitting in the Oval Office one day.

FYI

Here are three books for sharing on Presidents' Day:

Mr. President: A Book of U.S. Presidents, revised edition, by George Sullivan (New York: Scholastic, 1997). Easy-to-read essays on the lives of the presidents from Washington to Clinton.

Yo, Millard Fillmore! (And All Those Other Presidents You Don't Know) by Will Cleveland and Mark Alvarez, illustrated by Tate Nation (New York: Scholastic, 1993). Offers a fast, easy way to learn a little about the presidents with memory tricks for recalling them all.

A Picture Book of John F. Kennedy by David A. Adler, illustrated by Robert Casilla (New York: Holiday House, 1991). A strikingly illustrated book on President Kennedy's life and death.

Encourage your child to write a letter to the president. The White House staff usually responds. This lets your child experience a part of democratic government—being able to communicate directly with the head of state—that is a precious right.

If you celebrate Easter, Passover, or another spring religious holiday, teach your child about why the event is important to your family. At this time of year, some youth groups encourage exchanges where kids from different faiths take part in each other's traditions. Maybe you live in a community where you can involve your child in something like this. Take advantage of this chance for your child to learn more about her own religion as well as other peoples'.

Do you celebrate St. Patrick's Day, Cinco de Mayo, Syttende Mai, or another ethnic holiday? If so, keep the tradition alive for yourself and your child. Invite people who don't share your background to take part as well. These holidays offer a chance for families to learn about and appreciate other people's traditions.

Teach your child the meaning of Memorial Day. Tell him that Memorial Day was begun as a day to honor soldiers who had died in war. Explain that people now remember those men and women as well as others who are no longer living. As a family, you might want to visit the gravesites of loved ones who have died.

Take advantage of Memorial Day for a trip down memory lane. Share some family history with your son or daughter. Dig out the picture albums, home movies, and videos.

Help your child plan a simple Mother's or Father's Day gift. Tell your child that Mom or Dad might enjoy breakfast in bed, extra help with chores, or coupons to use later.

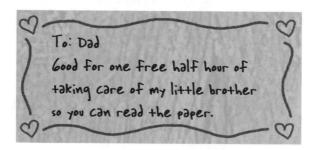

To: Dad
Good for one free half hour of taking care of my little brother so you can read the paper.

Tell your child that Independence Day is the nation's birthday. Discuss the history that led to independence.

Explain that Labor Day is a holiday to honor working people. Your child may be surprised to learn this. Talk about the different jobs workers do, from making and packaging food to building cars and airplanes.

If your child needs to brush up on school skills, talk to the teacher. Together, you can plan a way to keep your child learning and developing skills over the extended break. The teacher might suggest summer school. Or, he might suggest workbooks or other materials for you to use with your child.

Summer is a great time to start a journal. Buy your child a spiral tablet or blank book. You might say, "You can use this book to draw or write about all your summer adventures, or to keep busy when you're looking for something to do." If your child wants the journal to be private, respect that. Children need to be able to record thoughts they don't want to share with anyone else. Keeping a journal inspires your child to practice writing, to think about and solve problems, and to be creative.

FYI

Help your daughter discover the joys of journaling with one of these books written by teen author Jessica Wilber:

The Absolutely True, Positively Awesome Book About . . . Me!!! (Minneapolis: Free Spirit Publishing, 1999) is for girls ages 6–10. *Totally Private & Personal: Journaling Ideas for Girls and Young Women* (Minneapolis: Free Spirit Publishing, 1996) is for girls 11 and up. The author draws on her own years of journaling experience to offer ideas for keeping a journal and feeling good about being a girl.

Give your child a tour of your state or province. Visit a local welcome center where your child can pick up brochures about attractions across the state. Use the brochures to plan outings. You might aim to go on one trip to a different region each year.

Include your child in making vacation plans. Together, plan and reserve campsites or motel rooms. Have your child write for state, provincial, or national park brochures. Use the library or the Internet to research the places you'll visit.

Get an extra road map for your child when you travel. Highlight your route and explain what some of the map symbols mean. This will help your child stay busy and practice geography skills, and the trip may not seem so long.

FYI

Here's a travel journal that will keep boys and girls busy and involved:

The Travel Bug: A Travel Journal for Kids 7 to 14 by Linda Schwartz, illustrated by Bev Armstrong (Santa Barbara, CA: The Learning Works, 1993). Helps kids get ready to travel, learn about the places they visit, and remember all the fun.

When traveling to different regions, explain the scenery. For example, point out all the wheat or soybean fields and talk about the foods made from each crop. Compare a flat tableland to mountains viewed in the distance. As you pass an industrialized area, talk about the products and jobs that industry provides.

If you won't be taking a trip, plan an at-home vacation instead. Visit a few local sites like the zoo, museum, or park. Take hikes. Jog or bike the local trails. Don't forget to balance your time exploring with time for just hanging out together as a family.

If you have a camera, teach your child to use it. Then turn her loose on a family trip or at a neighborhood picnic. After the pictures are developed, your child may want to mount the pictures in a scrapbook, label and date them, and write notes or captions.

Enroll your child in lessons or camp. This doesn't have to be expensive. Many schools, libraries, and museums offer summer programs in everything from foreign languages to computers to drama. YMCAs, YWCAs, scouting programs, and parks offer plenty of outdoor learning activities. If your budget is tight, ask about scholarships or sliding fees.

Make it a goal for your daughter or son to develop at least one new skill over the summer break. Support your child in working toward it. For example, if your son is learning to swim, take him to the pool and help him practice his strokes. If your daughter's taking guitar lessons, help her set aside time and follow through with practicing every day.

Flex your child's mental muscles: turn the TV to an educational channel or turn it off altogether.

Give your child the gift of downtime. Many lifelong childhood memories of summer come from simple pleasures like catching lightning bugs, playing outdoors, or building a tent from sheets. Quiet time spent reading, dreaming, and listening to music is also good for your child.

Just as we cherish long summer days, cherish the moments with your child. In the hustle of everyday life, remind yourself how lucky you are to be blessed with the love and laughter of a child. The years pass by quickly; take some time to savor them along the way.

Index

A

absences, 35, 44
Absolutely True, Positively Awesome Book About...Me!!! (Wilber), 190
accidents at school, 59
Agendamate, 37
anger, excessive, 163
apologizing, 151
artwork, 99, 127
Ask Jeeves for Kids (Web site), 78
attitudes
 parents as models for, 11, 76, 155–156
 toward schoolwork, 39, 79–80
authority, respect for, 153

B

backpacks, 13, 44–45, 50
bathroom use, 58
beach activities, 124
bedtimes, 9, 44, 58
berry picking, 124
bird-watching, 125
birthday celebrations, 176–177
B.J. Pinchbeck's Homework Helper
 (Web site), 78
Black History Month, 185
body odor, 59
bullies, 161–162
Bullies Are a Pain in the Brain
 (Romain), 162
bus riding, 18–19

C

calculators, 85
calendars, 23, 50–51
camping, 125
Career Ideas for Kids Who Like Art
 (Reeves), 113
Career Ideas for Kids Who Like Science
 (Reeves), 113
Career Ideas for Kids Who Like Sports
 (Reeves & Bond), 113
Career Ideas for Kids Who Like Talking
 (Reeves & Heubeck), 113
career planning, 111–113
Child Connection, Inc. (Web site), 73

child development, 144
Child's Celebration of the World, 119
choices, offering, 138
chores, 138–139
Cobblestone magazine, 129
college planning, 112
commitments, keeping, 142–143
communicating
 with children, 45–47, 133, 159–160
 with other parents, 140, 142, 163
 with school personnel, 19–20, 37
 with teachers, 28–30, 32–34, 37–41,
  99–100, 145–146, 158–159
 when language differences exist, 28
computers, 125–126, 132, 141
conferences, 29–30, 33–34
conflicts, resolving, 37–38, 158–163
conservation, 122
conversation starters, 46–47
cooking, 130
coupon clipping, 130
crafts, 127
Cricket magazine, 129
current events, 120
customs, family/cultural, 22, 117, 176, 180

D

differences, appreciating and respecting,
 116–119, 154–155
disabilities, people with, 155, 157–158
disappointment, 137
Disaster Blasters (Kasdin &
 Szabo-Cohen), 72
discipline at school, 145
diversity, cultural, 116–119, 154–155
dress codes, 15–16
drug abuse, 63–64

E

eating, healthy, 56–57
emergency calls, 71
emergency contacts, 20–21
Every Child Can Succeed (Tobias), 96
exercise, 57
Explosive Child (Greene), 144
extracurricular activities, 94

F

family crises, 40
Father's Day, 188
Favorite Folktales from Around the World
   (Yolen), 140
field trips, paying for, 41
50 Nifty Super Science Experiments (Melton
   et al.), 89
fighting, 64, 163
*Finding Help When Your Child Is Struggling
   in School* (Greene), 100
fire safety, 67–69
First Thanksgiving (George), 179
flags, 118
folktales, 139–140
Food Guide Pyramid, 56
Footsteps magazine, 129
friends
   making, 8, 156–157
   visiting homes of, 72, 142, 156–157

G

games, 119, 126, 133
gardening, 121–122
getting up, 139
gifted children, 102–103
*Gifted Kids' Survival Guide For Ages 10 &
   Under* (Galbraith), 103
Gifted Kids' Survival Guide (Galbraith &
   Delisle), 103
gifts, giving, 181–182
goal setting, 108–111
grades and grading, 79, 81–82
guns, 64–65

H

Halloween, 177–178
helpfulness, encouraging, 146
holidays
   as catch-up time, 51, 189
   as a chance for quality time, 182
   gift exchanges, 181–183
   keeping children focused, 180
   from other cultures, 180
   religious/ethnic, 22, 187
   See also under specific holiday
homework
   assisting children with, 76–78, 80–81
   building confidence, 79–80
   completing, 36–37, 48–49, 76, 82–83
   helping with science and social
      studies, 87–89
   helping with spelling, 89–90
   strengthening math skills, 83–85
   strengthening reading skills, 85–87
   time spent on, 35–36
   See also schoolwork
Homework Central (Web site), 78
How to Do Homework Without Throwing Up
   (Romain), 81
How to Handle a Hard-to-Handle Kid
   (Edwards), 144
How to Help Your Child with Homework
   (Radencich & Schumm), 81

I

If You Sailed on the Mayflower in 1620
   (McGovern), 179
I Have a Dream (Davidson), 184
I Have a Dream (King & King), 184
illnesses/injuries
   keeping children home, 61–62
   responding safely to, 59
   taking children home, 20–21
immunizations, 21
Independence Day, 188
information, organizing key, 22–23
Internet, 126, 132, 141
invitations, 154
"I-statements," 159
Is Your Child Ready for First Grade?
   (Tilghman), 8

J

journaling, 189–191

K

kindergarten, 7–8
Kindergarten—Ready or Not? (Walmsley &
   Walmsley), 8
Kingfisher Young People's Atlas of the World
   (Steele), 119
knives, 64–65

L

labeling belongings, 13
Labor Day, 189
latchkey programs, 70–71

learning differences (LD), 100–101
Learning Differences Sourcebook (Boyles &
    Contadiono), 101
learning styles, 32, 95–96
leaving home, 9, 44
libraries, 25, 128
lice, 59
listening skills, 133
losing belongings, 13–14

M

magazines, 128–129, 172
mainstreamed classrooms, 157–158
manners, 150–154
Martin Luther King, Jr. Day, 183–184
math skills, strengthening, 83–85, 130–131
Mayberry, U.S.A. (Web site), 141
meal cards/money, safeguarding, 14
mealtimes, 53
medications and medical conditions,
    19–20, 62–63
Memorial Day, 187–188
menstrual periods, 59–60
misbehavior, 145–146, 163
mistakes, 96–97
Mother's Day, 188
movies, 131–132, 140–141
Mr. President (Sullivan), 186
Multiplication Motivation, 84
museums, 127
music, 131, 143

N

National Education Association (NEA)
    (Web site), 33
National Geographic World magazine, 129
nature walks, 123
newspapers, 120
99 Ways to Get Kids to Love Reading
    (Leonhardt), 87
"no-noise hours," 136
nutrition, 56–57

O

*101 Things Every Kid Should Know About
    Science* (Beres), 89
open houses, 24
Oppenheim Toy Portfolio, 1999 (Oppenheim
    et al.), 126

P

Parent's Handbook (Dinkmeyer et al.), 144
Parent Teacher Association (PTA), 169–170
Parent Teacher Student Organization
    (PTSO), 169–170
patriotism, 118
People (Spier), 119
persistence, 104–105
Picture Book of John F. Kennedy (Adler), 186
Picture Book of Martin Luther King, Jr.
    (Adler), 184
Playing Their Parts (Farkas et al.), 170
praise, giving, 98–99, 110
prejudices, 154–155
Presidents' Day, 185–187
puzzles, 128

Q

questions, asking, 46–47, 97, 133

R

Read All About It! (Trelease), 52
Read-Aloud Handbook (Trelease), 52
reading skills, strengthening, 85–87
reading time, 49, 51–52, 128
recycling, 122
religious practices, 22
respect, 149–150, 153
routines, 43–45, 48–50, 53
rules, setting, 137

S

safety
    on the bus, 19
    for children left alone, 67, 69–71
    equipment, 66
    fire, 67–69
    with fireworks, 64
    Halloween, 177
    in other children's homes, 72, 142
    with strangers, 73
    traveling to school, 19, 65–66, 67
    in weather emergencies, 69
school
    choice of, 6
    clothes for, 15–18, 60–61
    supplies for, 11–15, 51
School Survival Guide for Kids with LD
    (Cummings & Fisher), 101

School Testing (Gellman), 31
schoolwork
    attitudes toward, 39, 79–80
    checking, 49
    displaying, 99
    See also homework
science, helping with, 87–89
self-confidence, 79–80, 94
self-control, 136
service learning, 173
sharing, 154
social studies, helping with, 87–89
spelling, helping with, 89–90
Spider magazine, 129
sports, 121, 143
stargazing, 123
starting school, 6–8
substance abuse, 63–64
summer camp, 192
summer vacations
    appreciating, 193
    planning, 190–191, 192
    returning to school from, 9
    as a time for journaling, 189–191
    as a time for learning, 190–193
Survival Guide for Parents of Gifted Kids
    (Walker), 103
swimming, 67

T

talents, 94
teachable moments, 116
teachers
    adjusting to new, 10
    communicating with, 28–30, 32–34,
        37–41, 99–100
    expectations for, 10–11, 38
    expressing appreciation to, 41
    requesting specific, 6
Teaching Your Child to Be Home Alone
    (Grollman & Sweden), 72
teeth, loose, 59
television, 49, 131–132, 140–141
tests and testing, 30, 90–91
test scores, 30–31
Thanksgiving, 178–179
Totally Private & Personal (Wilber), 190
Traditions Around the World (Hall), 119
Travel Bug (Schwartz), 191

traveling to school, 18–19, 65–66, 67
True or False? Tests Stink! (Romain &
    Verdick), 91

U

Unglued from the Tube (Web site), 141
uniforms, 16–17
U.S. Department of Agriculture
    (Web site), 56

V

vacations. *See* summer vacations
Valentine's Day, 185
Veteran's Day, 178
violent behavior, 163
volunteering
    effective, 166–167, 172
    employer support for, 166, 171–172
    opportunities for, 168–171
volunteers
    children as, 173
    grandparents as, 167–168
    parents as, 166, 168–169, 172–173
voting, 120–121

W

weather emergencies, 69
Web sites
    Ask Jeeves for Kids, 78
    B.J. Pinchbeck's Homework Helper, 78
    Child Connection, Inc., 73
    Homework Central, 78
    Mayberry, U.S.A., 141
    National Education Association
        (NEA), 33
    Unglued from the Tube, 141
    U.S. Department of Agriculture, 56
We Can Get Along (Payne & Rohling), 162
What Do You Think? (Schwartz), 162
*What to Do...When Kids Are Mean to Your
    Child* (McCoy), 162
What Would You Do? (Schwartz), 69
*When Your Child Has LD (Learning
    Differences)* (Fisher &
    Cummings), 101

Y

Yo, Millard Fillmore! (Cleveland &
    Alvarez), 186

About the Authors

Rosemarie Clark, M.Ed., is a fourth-grade teacher at Overdale Elementary School in Louisville, Kentucky, where she also tutors individual students. Rosemarie has twelve years of teaching experience in both public and private schools, and lives in Louisville with her husband and sons.

Donna Hawkins, M.Ed., teaches science classes to students in grades 1–5 at Roby Elementary School in Shepherdsville, Kentucky. She has eight years of teaching experience in both public and private schools. Donna lives with her husband and three children in Shepherdsville.

Beth Vachon, M.Ed., is a fourth-grade teacher and writing coordinator at Overdale Elementary School in Louisville, Kentucky. Beth has eighteen years of teaching experience in public schools. She lives in Shepherdsville, Kentucky, with her husband and two daughters.

Clockwise from left: Rosemarie Clark,
Beth Vachon, Donna Hawkins.

Other Great Books from Free Spirit

What Young Children Need to Succeed

Working Together to Build Assets
from Birth to Age 11

by Jolene L. Roehlkepartain and Nancy Leffert, Ph.D.

This book explains how to build developmental assets—family support, positive values, social skills, and more—in four different age groups from birth to 11 years. For parents, teachers, community leaders, and children.

$8.95; 240 pp.; illus.; 5¼" x 8"

Playing Smart

A Parent's Guide to Enriching, Offbeat Learning Activities for Ages 4–14

by Susan K. Perry

Hundreds of fun, unconventional activities turn spare time into quality time with your child. You'll explore photography, cooking, cultural relativity, and more. Most activities require little or no preparation. For parents of children ages 4–14.

$14.95; 224 pp.; softcover; illus.; 7¼" x 9¼"

How to Help Your Child with Homework

Every Caring Parent's Guide to Encouraging Good Study Habits and Ending the Homework Wars

by Marguerite C. Radencich, Ph.D., and Jeanne Shay Schumm, Ph.D.

Put an end to excuses and arguments while improving your child's school performance. Realistic strategies and proven techniques make homework hassle-free. For parents of children ages 6–13.

$14.95; 208 pp.; softcover; 7¼" x 9¼"

To place an order or to request a free catalog of
SELF–HELP FOR KIDS® and SELF–HELP FOR TEENS®
materials, please write, call, email, or visit our Web site:

Free Spirit Publishing Inc.
400 First Avenue North • Suite 616 • Minneapolis, MN 55401-1724
toll-free 800.735.7323 • local 612.338.2068 • fax 612.337.5050
help4kids@freespirit.com • www.freespirit.com